BLOOMBERG'S HIDDEN LEGACY

Climate Change and the Future of New York City

Katherine Bagley & Maria Gallucci

ISBN-13: 9780692224908
ISBN-10: 0692224904
Library of Congress Control Number: 2014909634
CreateSpace Independent Publishing Platform
North Charleston, South Carolina

TABLE OF CONTENTS

1

THE STORM

On the night of Oct. 29, 2012, Mayor Michael Bloomberg hunkered down in the command room of New York City's Operations and Emergency Management headquarters, waiting for the full force of Superstorm Sandy to hit. Hurricane-force winds were ripping across the city, tearing trees from their roots and snapping utility poles in half. Surges of water turned streets into rivers, flooding subway tunnels and washing away homes, storefronts and cars.

City, state, federal officials, utility company representatives— all were typing furiously on laptops, phones pressed against their ears, trying to figure out what was happening and where, who was in danger and how.

A vending machine cranked out cereal bars and potato chips. Dirty coffee cups piled up. Giant, flat-screen TVs on every wall flashed images of rising floodwaters and heavy winds wreaking havoc outside the command center. Phones rang incessantly. Computers hummed and whirred.

In the middle of it all was Bloomberg, absorbing the news and conferring with his top officials about what to do next, how to respond.

At 7:30 p.m., they got the news they'd been bracing for: Sandy had made landfall.

Bloomberg and his staff knew enough about the city's vulnerability to flooding and storm surge to know that the end of this particular New York story would be bad.

Local scientists had predicted for at least 15 years that the changing climate would bring rising sea levels and more dangerous storms to the city's 520 miles of coastlines. But little had been done to prepare for these dangers until 2007, during Bloomberg's second term, when his administration launched what it hoped would become the world's most comprehensive sustainability agenda, PlaNYC.

They still weren't ready for a storm like the one that was raging outside. They simply hadn't had the time or the focus or the money to do it all, to truly protect New York from the impacts of climate change.

The storm's center struck just below Atlantic City, N.J., some 120 miles away. But it packed so much power that it felt like Sandy had slammed directly into New York.

A record 14-foot storm surge devoured the southern tip of Manhattan and entire waterfront neighborhoods in Brooklyn, Staten Island and Queens. Manhattan's glittering skyline went dark below 34th Street after the salty waters claimed an electrical substation. Nearly 100 million gallons of water rushed into the Brooklyn-Battery Tunnel, a toll road beneath the East River.

Patients on stretchers and hooked to IV bags were being evacuated where hospital emergency generators had failed. Fire was devouring entire blocks of homes in Breezy Point, in the Rockaway Peninsula in Queens.

Scott and Stacey Nagel watched in stunned silence from the front window of their home in Rockaway's Belle Harbor neighborhood. The water raced down the streets and crept up lawns and driveways. The power was out, but the sky still glowed bright from another fire burning just six blocks away, on Beach 130th Street. A call to the fire department confirmed what the Nagels already knew: all the roads were underwater. There was no getting on, off or around the peninsula.

Bloomberg had urged people in vulnerable neighborhoods to evacuate the night before, but many stayed behind. The Nagels fled their house in 2011 when Hurricane Irene threatened to pummel the city, and nothing had happened. What was the point in leaving this time? Now, they watched the nearby flames with alarm. If the fire reached their house, where would they go?

At about 9 p.m., Bloomberg held a news conference in a small meeting room. He had traded the black jacket, white oxford shirt and purple tie he wore that morning for a crisp blue dress shirt. In his trademark monotone, he updated New Yorkers on the damage Sandy was causing. Drivers should stay off the roads, he said. People should stay away from windows. Everyone should shelter in place.

"Do not go outside. It is still very dangerous," he cautioned. He pleaded with residents to call 911 only for life-threatening emergencies. The system was fielding 10,000 calls per half hour. "These are not games. We've said from the very beginning, this is a once-in-a-long-time storm," he said from behind the podium.

Cynthia Rosenzweig watched the news from her 97-year-old mother's house near Tarrytown, a village just north of Manhattan. Rosenzweig, a senior scientist at the NASA Goddard Institute for Space Studies, was one of the first researchers to warn of the dangers climate change posed for New York.

That night she stepped outside her mother's house to check her car and was blasted by gale-force winds. At that moment, in the dark, she saw the clear link between Sandy and her life's work.

Others who had worked with Bloomberg on PlaNYC rode out the storm from their own homes. A brownstone in Brooklyn's Park Slope neighborhood, where whole trees cracked and fell. An apartment building in lower Manhattan, without power and surrounded by water. A riverfront house just north of the city, where two feet of water flooded the first floor.

Rit Aggarwala, who had helped create PlaNYC, watched from Palo Alto, Calif., where he'd lived with his wife for the past two years. He swiped his smartphone incessantly to get the latest news from New York.

"We knew this was coming, we just didn't know it would come so soon," he said later. "Most of what PlaNYC had included for climate change adaptation was still not yet at a point where it would make much difference."

As Monday slipped into Tuesday, the worst of the storm passed. Houses lay in ruins, filled with water or crumpling into piles of debris. Apartment towers were dark, without water, without heat. Streets, bridges and subway tunnels had vanished under water.

The Nagels watched from their window until the flames on Beach 130th Street finally died and the ocean waters began to recede. Their basement was flooded with seven feet of water, but at least the house hadn't caught fire. They shuffled upstairs to their bedroom and tried to sleep.

The mayor stayed at the Brooklyn Heights command center until the early hours of Tuesday morning. A few hours later, he was in a helicopter, surveying the most heavily damaged areas: the Rockaways, lower Manhattan, Staten Island, Coney Island, Brighton Beach and Howard Beach.

When he got back to the command center, a buffet lunch was being served. But few people sat down to eat. Most had spent the night in the building, sleeping on cots. Now, fueled by adrenaline and caffeine, they were scrambling to put the broken city back together.

The mayor had talked with President Barack Obama on the phone that morning. They had discussed the nagging question everyone was asking: Was a storm like Sandy, so powerful and rare, a result of climate change?

There was no clear answer just yet. But Bloomberg and his team knew one thing for sure. The plans they had crafted over the past five years were only the crude beginning of what the city needed. Sandy showed them they had to do much more, much faster.

2

THINK BIG

In the fall of 2006, Michael Bloomberg was comfortably installed in New York City Hall, a two-century-old building near the mouth of the Brooklyn Bridge, just blocks from Wall Street. He was a year into his second term as mayor and his approval ratings hovered above 70 percent. The economy was flourishing. Crime and poverty rates were down. For the first time since the 2001 terrorist attacks, New Yorkers were happy and the city was thriving.

But Bloomberg had never been one to sit back and enjoy a slow period. His restless mind was always searching for big challenges, big ideas—the kind of idea he was preparing to reveal in just a few weeks.

The plan had begun taking shape a year earlier, when the city's demographers had come up with a startling forecast: By 2030, a million more people would likely be living in New York, boosting the city's population to nine million.

New York was already bursting at the seams. Parks were overcrowded. Roadways were clogged with traffic. Subways and buses often exceeded their carrying capacities, particularly during rush hours. Air pollution levels were high and childhood asthma rates were rising. Land was so precious that city agencies were struggling to find places to store salt piles for winter road maintenance or to park off-duty garbage trucks.

The city needed a plan to cope with the coming crush, and in 2005 Dan Doctoroff, Bloomberg's deputy mayor for economic development and rebuilding, had begun putting one together. As Doctoroff and his staff studied the problem, they realized that environmental issues needed to be factored in, too. Pollution had to be reduced, energy efficiency improved and greenhouse gas emissions cut. They needed to look at the growing city from a new perspective, a sustainability perspective.

"Sustainability" was already a popular buzzword in 2006, a term used to indicate some degree of environmental consciousness. In its biggest, grandest philosophical form, sustainability meant using resources wisely to sustain life on earth. It could be as simple as installing low-flow toilets, or as complex as redesigning buildings to guzzle less energy. For New York, it meant figuring out how to balance rapid growth with preserving the environment and quality of life.

In some ways, Bloomberg was uniquely qualified to steer the city into this uncharted territory. He'd always been interested in science, so thinking about the environment was natural to him. As a boy he'd hung out at the Boston Museum of Science and roamed his family garden. At Johns Hopkins University, he studied physics before switching to electrical engineering.

In his first term as mayor, however, his environmental credentials were mixed.

He had spearheaded a land-buying campaign in the Catskill Mountains to protect the source of the city's drinking water. He'd also waged a political battle to refigure the city's garbage collection system, improving air quality in the process.

On the other hand, he had temporarily suspended the city's plastic recycling program to help balance the budget. And despite a series of reports warning of the risks climate change posed to the city, he—like Rudy Giuliani before him—hadn't shown much inclination to take action.

Now, with the city in better shape and the stress of a reelection campaign behind him, Bloomberg was ready to embrace more environmental initiatives. The plan he was preparing to make public had begun as a traditional land use analysis and evolved into a sweeping sustainability agenda. Over the next six years, it would become bigger yet: an aggressive climate change action plan that would transform New York and the mayor into world leaders on global warming at a time when many U.S. politicians were doing their best to avoid the controversial topic.

Doctoroff, the instigator of the project, had risen from little-known Wall Street investment banker to one of the city's top political movers and shakers remarkably fast, even by New York standards.

He'd begun networking his way through New York's top political circles in the mid-1990s, when he was a partner at a private equity firm and launched an effort to bring the 2012 Summer Olympics to New York City. Bloomberg, the billionaire owner of the financial data company Bloomberg L.P., donated money to the effort and sat on the planning board.

Like most New Yorkers, however, Doctoroff's priorities changed on Sept. 11, 2001, when terrorists struck the twin World Trade Center towers. Businesses fled to nearby Connecticut or New Jersey. Within a year, nearly 35 percent of Battery City, a cluster of office and residential high-rises in lower Manhattan, lay vacant. The city was ravaged emotionally, physically and economically.

Mourning New Yorkers elected Bloomberg, a novice politician, as their new mayor partly because he promised to use his business expertise to revitalize the crippled city. In his campaign, Bloomberg had used many of the projects Doctoroff had proposed for the Olympics—things like expanding subway services and developing the waterfront—to illustrate his vision for New York. So it seemed natural to ask Doctoroff to be his deputy mayor for economic development and rebuilding.

Doctoroff turned down the offer—twice.

"I had a private equity firm I was leading. I was leading the Olympic bid. My father was very sick. So I said no," Doctoroff recalled.

Finally, Bloomberg invited him to a one-on-one meeting and argued that as deputy mayor, Doctoroff could work on many of the initiatives he had created for the Olympics even if the city failed to win the bid. Doctoroff emerged 90 minutes later agreeing to take the job.

Doctoroff settled into a desk just eight feet from the mayor in the Bullpen, a humming cluster of about 50 cubicles that sits beneath crystal chandeliers on the second floor of City Hall. The room, set up to resemble a financial trading floor, is considered the nerve center of the Bloomberg administration, with the mayor famously situated not in the traditional corner office, but squarely in the middle, in a cubicle of his own.

Doctoroff began meeting with the commissioners who reported to him—planning, environmental protection, transportation, finance and housing—as well as a few who didn't. Dubbed the Economic Development Agency Council, they met one Wednesday a month at 110 William Street, seven blocks south of City Hall.

It was at one of those meetings that Doctoroff learned of the coming population boom from city demographers. Like everyone in the room, he was stunned.

"It didn't take a huge leap of imagination to understand that if the city was already crowded, how much worse it would be if the population grew," Doctoroff said. "That ultimately became the most important call to action. We know what it's like today in this cramped city. What would it be like" with another million New Yorkers?

In 2005, New York City lost the Olympics bid to London, and the project that had consumed Doctoroff's life for a decade no longer required his attention.

"It freed up a bit of capacity in Dan's mind," said Marc Ricks, an infrastructure expert who served as Doctoroff's chief of staff. "He is a remarkable force when he has the mind share to dedicate to something. Suddenly, the scope can expand, the aspirations can grow and a lot can happen."

With the Olympics gone, Doctoroff focused on preparing the city for the projected population growth. He decided to develop a strategic land use plan and ask each city agency to formally assess how an extra million people would affect its operations.

Some agencies pushed back against doing the additional work. Others were eager to participate.

"For the most part, people were amazingly cooperative," Doctoroff said. "Given the number of people we had, that was shocking."

The reports showed that the population boom would dangerously strain the city's roads, transit systems, water systems and energy supplies. Air, water and environmental quality would deteriorate. And where, exactly, would those extra million people be housed when most of the city's land was already occupied?

A sense of urgency energized their work. Doctoroff dedicated more staff and more resources to figuring out how to grow the city responsibly while maintaining, or even improving, quality of life. He drove them hard. The team started meeting on Sundays, on their own time. The deeper they dug, the more alarmed they became.

While Doctoroff focused on land use issues, New York's scientific and environmental communities were worrying about climate change. They had already spent a decade researching sustainability issues and the potential impacts of global warming on the region. But their efforts were scattered and lacked leadership. Scientists conducted research, environmentalists produced reports, but in the end, they couldn't grab the attention of the public or politicians.

In the mid-1990s a report by policy experts and scientists, "The Baked Apple? Metropolitan New York in the Greenhouse," laid out which parts of the city were vulnerable to climate change and exactly how they would be affected. That report was followed by the Environmental Defense Fund's "Hot Nights in the City: Global Warming, Sea-level Rise and the New York Metropolitan Region," which looked at how climate change would drive up things like heat-stress mortality, mosquito-borne disease and asthma cases.

But the warnings were ignored. Then-mayor Rudy Giuliani and city officials argued that if action was indeed necessary, it could be delayed, because climate change was a long-term problem.

In 1997, the scientists had a glimmer of hope when President Bill Clinton said he would prioritize climate change during his second term.

The Intergovernmental Panel on Climate Change, the United Nations-run scientific authority on global warming, had published its second report, and evidence was mounting that human activities were dangerously altering the climate.

"I know not everyone agrees on how to interpret the scientific conclusions," Clinton said. "But I think we all have to agree that the potential for serious climate disruption is real. It would clearly be a grave mistake to bury our heads in the sand and pretend the issue will go away."

The Clinton administration launched a national assessment to evaluate the country's vulnerability to global climate change, splitting the U.S. into 18 study regions. The assessment for the New York area was led by Columbia University's Earth Institute, a campus-wide collaboration of scientists, engineers and policy experts aimed at solving global environmental issues.

Cynthia Rosenzweig, an agricultural scientist at NASA's Goddard Institute for Space Studies, a partner of the Earth Institute, co-led the project with Bill Solecki, a policy and planning expert then at Montclair State University in New Jersey.

Rosenzweig and Solecki gathered more than a dozen scientists at universities across the region and invited representatives from city, regional and federal agencies to contribute. The report that emerged, the "Metropolitan East Coast Assessment: Climate Change and a Global City," covered 31 counties in New York, New Jersey and Connecticut.

It addressed how rising seas, stronger storms and heat caused by climate change would affect coasts, wetlands, transportation, water supplies, energy and public health. The scientists hoped that because city agencies had participated in the research, political leaders would finally wake up to the urgent need to address global warming.

They set a publication date of September 12, 2001—the day after terrorists flew airplanes into the World Trade Center towers, killing 2,753 people.

The Port Authority of New York and New Jersey, one of the major collaborators on the climate report, was based in the North Tower. It was days before Rosenzweig and Solecki learned that the people they'd been working with for years had survived.

The report was released the following spring, but it was largely ignored by city agencies and the newly installed Bloomberg administration.

"For almost five years, you couldn't talk with anybody [in city government] about anything other than terrorism," said Klaus Jacob, a geophysicist at Columbia University who contributed to the report. "We lost five years to work on climate and other risks."

Still, the scientists continued producing reports about climate change, about the vulnerability of New York's transportation system, about the other dangers that lay ahead. With each study, they tried—and generally failed—to get officials to take notice.

Year after year, study after study, their frustration grew. Other U.S. scientists shared that frustration. With President George W. Bush in office, there was little productive conversation about climate change at the federal level. The Intergovernmental Panel on Climate Change had released a third report, warning again that increasing greenhouse gas emissions could be catastrophic for communities around the globe. Yet Congress and the Bush administration weren't convinced that aggressive action was needed. The few measures they did take, like creating a clean-energy loan program, were couched in terms of promoting energy independence.

"Everybody was feeling vaguely impotent about [national action]," said Marcia Bystryn, president of the New York League of Conservation Voters, a powerful environmental policy group. Like other environmentalists, she was coming to the conclusion that cities were the best places to address climate change.

"That's where the bulk of CO_2 emissions come from, and cities have a capacity to affect that," she said. "Cities can get things done."

Some cities were already jumping on the bandwagon and launching sustainability and climate change initiatives. London created "The London Plan" that included planning guides for sustainable construction, energy, air quality and waste. San Francisco, Seattle, Portland, Ore. and Toronto implemented similar strategies.

Bystryn and other New York environmentalists saw a unique opportunity for their city to lead this wave, if only they could persuade their politicians to listen.

Green groups aggressively lobbied New York City officials and politicians to address the issue. In June 2005, City Councilman James Gennaro, a trained geologist who chairs the council's environmental protection committee, authored a bill asking the city to reduce greenhouse gas emissions by 20 percent. But Gennaro said it was "unembraced by the Bloomberg administration," which argued that the legislation overly simplified a complex task. The bill never made it to a vote.

The city's energy policy taskforce predicted that energy demand would outpace supply in the next 10 years, but it didn't spell out how New York could solve the problem. In 2004, a citywide interagency sustainability taskforce was created, but it never made any recommendations.

Bloomberg's interest in climate change was deepening, however.

After the United States refused to sign the Kyoto Protocol, an international agreement to reduce carbon emissions, he joined a coalition of mayors who promised their cities would meet the Protocol's emission targets.

In a commencement speech at Johns Hopkins University School of Medicine, Bloomberg publicly defended climate science—an unusual step for a Republican given that many of the party's leaders were questioning whether the earth was warming.

"Despite near-unanimity in the science community, there's now a movement driven by ideology and short-term economics to ignore the evidence and discredit the reality of climatic change," he told the graduates.

As the end of his first term approached in 2005, Bloomberg had become a vocal leader on climate change. But his commitment was still only verbal. His administration had yet to take direct action.

3

ASSEMBLE THE TEAM

Rohit Aggarwala knew next to nothing about the debate brimming in New York City over how to accommodate a million more New Yorkers by 2030. The 34-year-old transportation buff, who goes by Rit, was a rising star at the global consulting behemoth McKinsey & Company. He was working on a big project and starting the run to make partner.

Still, Aggarwala was intrigued by the call he got in March 2006 from Marc Ricks, a former McKinsey colleague who was now Deputy Mayor Dan Doctoroff's chief of staff. For more than six months, Doctoroff had been creating a strategic land use plan to accommodate the extra people. But the project had become so complex that he and Bloomberg decided it needed its own staff and office. Would Aggarwala consider leading the transportation piece of the plan, Ricks asked?

"As an intellectual challenge, what could be more appealing for somebody who was interested in transportation, who is from New York and loves New York?" Aggarwala said, looking back at the chain of events that pulled him into Bloomberg's fold.

Still, Aggarwala wasn't convinced the job was right for him. Joining the Bloomberg administration would put the brakes on his career at McKinsey. Plus, he'd worked in politics before, first as a transportation policy advisor to a Democratic assemblyman in Albany, and later in the

U.S. Department of Transportation during the Clinton administration. "It's not the same as being at a consulting firm where you know that just by...doing your job and working hard you will be successful," he said.

A few weeks later, Aggarwala met with Doctoroff and Ricks at New York's City Hall. He rattled off his concerns about the position. Were they willing to take on the unpopular initiatives needed to keep New York a livable, thriving city? Were they ready, for example, to consider the controversial idea of congestion pricing, where drivers would pay a fee to enter parts of Manhattan during rush hour? London had adopted such a plan in 2003, but Bloomberg had brushed off the idea for New York.

"And Dan throws up his hands, and he says, 'We're already crunching the numbers!'" Aggarwala remembered.

Aggarwala walked out of City Hall 90 percent sure he would take the job. Doctoroff and Ricks were sure of something else. Aggarwala was more than a transit wonk. He was well versed in project management and knew how to whittle down ideas and put them into practice. They decided to refine their offer: They wanted Aggarwala to take over from Doctoroff and lead the entire long-term planning office, not just its transportation component.

In May, Aggarwala accepted the city's offer to head the newly created Office of Long-Term Planning.

Before his official start date in June, Aggarwala began attending the Sunday strategy sessions Doctoroff was holding at City Hall. He brought himself up to speed on the progress city agencies had already made on the strategic land use plan, including an initiative to outfit nearly 200 schoolyards with jungle gyms, athletic courts, benches and trees.

Many of the yards were concrete lots that teachers used for parking. Turning them into welcoming spaces would benefit the kids and the neighborhoods while also improving air quality. Getting the education and parks departments to collaborate had been tough, though, because the agencies rarely worked together.

Aggarwala pored over long-term plans and sustainability agendas fi other cities. He drew inspiration from climate action plans by Chicago ai Portland, Ore., and from a London program to retrofit commercial build ings for energy efficiency. He was particularly impressed by Santa Monica's sustainability plan. The California city laid out eight broad goals, each with a set of indicators to gauge the impact of the various programs.

Aggarwala also studied regional climate change reports that had generally been ignored over the years, particularly those by researchers at the NASA Goddard Institute for Space Studies, Columbia University and other regional universities. After work one day he caught a screening of "An Inconvenient Truth," the movie version of former Vice President Al Gore's campaign to educate the world about global warming. It had hit theaters a few months earlier, and the press and public were abuzz with chatter about it.

Until this point, environmental and climate issues had been only a peripheral part of the Bloomberg administration's long-term planning process. The primary focus had been on land use issues, including public parks, housing and contaminated industrial sites known as brownfields. Sustainability issues like air quality, water quality and greenhouse gas emissions had been discussed, but nothing had stuck quite yet.

After a couple of months in the trenches, however, Aggarwala began to see that sustainability wasn't just a side issue. Sustainability was as important to the city's development as land use issues. By July 1, Aggarwala was signing his emails the "director of long-term planning and sustainability" even though the office hadn't yet formally adopted the name.

Sustainability wasn't just about making scarce resources last longer or reducing environmental impact, Aggarwala and his team of six were discovering—it was also about making life better and healthier for the millions of people who live in the city. Enabling them to take the bus, ride their bikes and produce their own rooftop solar power; designing more efficient buildings and water networks; drastically cutting back on waste—all these steps would benefit the environment, as well as the growing city.

More than three-dozen sustainability initiatives were already underway in areas such as green buildings, energy efficiency and emissions reduction. But they were being rolled out quietly, and the agencies involved weren't coordinating their efforts.

ᵣuiding the ship. No one had pulled it all together
 ᵖlan," said Ariella Maron, who joined Aggarwala's team
policy advisor. That task would fall to her and her new
 ⸱ᵤes.

Convincing Bloomberg that the plan should be broadened to
include sustainability was easy, given the mayor's passion for sweeping
public health initiatives. Bloomberg had already banned smoking in
public spaces and would soon stop restaurants from using artery-clog-
ging artificial trans fats. Sustainability initiatives—like replacing dirty
heating oil with cleaner blends to drive down asthma rates, or building grassy parks to promote healthier lifestyles—fit perfectly with his
priorities.

"You can argue environment and public health is sort of the same
thing," Bloomberg told InsideClimate News in September in an hour-
long interview overlooking the Bullpen. The "pro-environmental stuff
may come from that as much as anything else."

As he talked about his administration's sustainability and climate
charge work, Bloomberg leaned back comfortably in his chair, absent-
mindedly slipping his loafers off and on.

As the plan shaped up, Aggarwala and his team faced the formidable
task of getting cooperation from more than a dozen city agencies that
often acted more like fiefdoms than branches of the same tree. They
also needed the backing of broad swaths of New Yorkers if their agenda
was going to survive outside City Hall. Critics, supporters and skeptics
needed to sit at the same table and have a voice in the plan.

One of the things Doctoroff had learned from his failed attempt
to bring the Olympics to New York was that public participation was
essential. He and Aggarwala were determined not to make the mistake
of steamrolling ahead with their proposals. (The plan's critics later saw
this as a marketing ploy to sell the plan to the public.)

To open the door wider, Aggarwala and his staff created a
Sustainability Advisory Board, a group of 17 leaders who represented

the city's myriad voices. Board members would meet regularly with Aggarwala's office and city staff to mull ideas and craft proposals.

The New York League of Conservation Voters, which had been urging the Bloomberg administration to create such a group, was among the five environmental organizations invited to join. So was Robert Yaro, president of the Regional Plan Association and a prominent opponent of Doctoroff's Olympic stadium proposal, and Ed Ott, executive director of the Central Labor Council, an umbrella group of New York's labor unions. Two City Council members—environmental chair James Gennaro and Speaker Christine Quinn—also joined.

The process was designed to keep ideas flowing and not box anyone into a corner. Board members would provide Aggarwala's office with feedback and advice, but the city wouldn't be obligated to use their suggestions. The members, in turn, wouldn't be required to endorse the final plan. All the board's discussions would be kept secret so members could trade ideas without creating a frenzy of speculation in the media. They didn't even distribute handouts at the meetings.

The Bloomberg team also wanted to make sure that anything they did on climate change was rooted in scientific data. So they arranged a partnership with the same group of scientists that had already spent nearly a decade studying climate change's regional impacts. Cynthia Rosenzweig, Bill Solecki and their colleagues would provide the administration with the latest research. Perhaps most important, they'd explain it on a pro-bono basis to city staffers.

By fall, Aggarwala and his team saw that the line between strategic land-use and sustainability had almost disappeared. Sustainability, which in the spring had seemed like only one slice of a larger pie, touched every part of the plan—it was the thread that tied all of the strategy's themes together. The office was formally named the Office of Long-Term Planning and Sustainability.

"Sustainability was actually at the heart of what we were talking about all along," Maron said.

The shift was so complete that some projects the staff had been considering were eliminated, because they didn't fit in the context of sustainability. Plans to lease or sell city-owned lands, to improve access to technology and services for senior citizens were dropped from the agenda.

On Sept. 21, 2006, Bloomberg announced publicly that his administration was trying to make New York one of the world's most sustainable cities.

Instead of making the announcement from the steps of City Hall, Bloomberg spoke at a California plant that manufactures environmentally friendly fuel cells. California Gov. Arnold Schwarzenegger, a globally recognized climate advocate, shared the stage with him.

The two prominent Republicans called for stronger efforts to reduce U.S. greenhouse gas emissions. They complained that President Bush had failed to take meaningful action on climate change.

"We don't wait for the federal government to take the leadership position ... we take the lead," Schwarzenegger said.

"I'm trying to go around the country and support those who have the vision to take this country forward and those who are not going to fall into the trap of partisan politics and ... gridlock," Bloomberg said. "The reality of climate change is incontrovertible, and the responsibility of all of us to address this is undeniable. There's no reason for [New York] to delay doing what we can and must do."

Then Bloomberg announced the creation of the sustainability office as well as the 17-member advisory board. The office would create an inventory to track the city's greenhouse gas emissions, Bloomberg said—"the largest such study ever undertaken by any local jurisdiction in our nation" and a critical tool for measuring the city's progress on climate change.

Such measurements would be important throughout the PlaNYC process. "We have a saying in the city that if you can't measure it, you can't fix it," the mayor often says. "You have to have the metrics."

Bloomberg and Aggarwala's team thought the sustainability plan could be completed sometime before Thanksgiving that year. They wanted to get the plan out fast, so they could get their projects started before Bloomberg's second term ended.

A week after the California tour, the mayor stopped by the first meeting of the Sustainability Advisory Board. It marked the start of a rare experiment in New York City politics: seating contentious industry, business and environmental interests at the same table to work toward the same goal.

"Each of you are here for one reason and one reason only—because we thought you were the best ones for the job. I don't know who you voted for, I don't care. I don't care where you come from or what you're doing—are you the best person?" Bloomberg said in his typically brusque style.

He thanked board members for volunteering their time. "They are volunteers, right? We can't afford to pay them," he joked—and jetted out of the room.

Andy Darrell, an advisory board member who attended the first meeting, sensed the excitement in the room.

"We all realized that if we're really going to make a difference, we're going to have to get all of these different sectors to work together," said Darrell, who is the New York regional director of the Environmental Defense Fund, a national advocacy group.

But other board members still didn't fully trust the city agencies they were supposed to advise. The public and private sectors had long been at odds over environmental policy, Ariella Maron recalled. "Every time some of the green organizations [proposed] legislation to City Council, you'd have people within the city at the agency level saying, 'no, no, no.'"

The mayor's comments in California and his appearance at the meeting helped break some of the ice, said Marcia Bystryn, who represented the New York League of Conservation Voters on the advisory board.

"You knew that it was something that not just some department was interested in, but the mayor was interested in," she said. "In city government, if you're not convinced the mayor is behind an initiative, you probably don't spend a lot of time on it, because you know it's just never going to have any real traction."

The full advisory board met once every three weeks with the participating city agencies. In between, subgroups focused on seven specific areas: energy efficiency and green buildings, energy supply and distribution, transportation, green infrastructure, land use and brownfields, waste management and climate change adaptation.

Consultants from McKinsey & Company, Aggarwala's former employer, helped organize the meetings and supplied background research on topics like energy supply and air quality. McKinsey's paid role in the process sparked accusations that the consulting giant created the plan, not the people of New York—a claim Aggarwala sharply rejects.

The mayor didn't meddle with the emerging plan. Doctoroff, Aggarwala and other city staffers "really were the…impetus behind pulling it all together," Bloomberg said in an interview. He trusted Doctoroff and gave him a lot of leeway.

At the Sunday meetings at City Hall, tempers were beginning to flare and frustrations were kicking in. Everyone was tired and working long hours, sometimes from sunrise to sunset. They had missed the Thanksgiving deadline. Now they were just trying to finish by the end of the year.

"We were all fighting over the future of our city," Aggarwala said, looking back on those stressful days. "These were people who by-and-large had lived their lives and planned to die in this city. So inevitably it was more passionate. Which was fascinating, and great. But it was exhausting."

By December, the sustainability office and its advisory board had held more than 100 hours of meetings. Not a word of their discussions had been leaked to the media.

"I'm not sure even Dan [Doctoroff] fully understood just how important those detailed working sessions were, because we developed enough of a good relationship with the advisory board that we could be fully off the record," Aggarwala said. "We talked about third-rail issues, many of which didn't make it into the plan, but stuff that would've been newsworthy if it had simply been reported that we had had a conversation about it."

The sustainability staff also met with roughly 50 community organizations to hear their ideas and share the proposals that were beginning to take shape. Even so, plenty of groups felt excluded from the conversation.

"We weren't asked to the table," Miquela Craytor, then-deputy director of Sustainable South Bronx, an urban environmental justice group, said of the PlaNYC process. She later remarked that "often these great new ideas are shoved down people's throats, and that's not a way to make something work."

Overall, however, the process seemed to be going well.

"We didn't have to be against anything. We could be part of the discussion about what are you for?" said Ed Ott, the advisory board member from the Central Labor Council. "I have never been involved in anything in the city where there are so many different organizations involved that wasn't acrimonious."

The scientists who were advising the office on climate change research were similarly encouraged. Their meetings with the city staffers made them feel their message was finally being heard and incorporated into the city's plans.

The long-term plan was swelling into something so complex and ambitious that it was clear it couldn't be finished by the end of the year. They had set 10 goals, but they were still determining which initiatives were needed to meet those targets.

The deadline kept shifting further down the road, until the only firm deadline was "as soon as possible."

To give the public a taste of what was going on, the sustainability team decided to announce the 10 "aggressive but achievable" goals and invite the public to weigh in.

On Dec. 10, 2006 the city bought ad space in local newspapers to announce the targets. The ads contained something Aggarwala considered remarkable—a column listing the names of all 17 members of the Sustainability Advisory Board, which had voluntarily endorsed the goals. "By and large, we managed to create consensus," he said.

Two days later, with typical Bloomberg pomp-and-circumstance, the mayor announced the 10 goals to hundreds of environmental and community leaders at the Queens Museum of Art, a pavilion built for the 1939 World's Fair. His communications staff had given the project a name: PlaNYC 2030.

Meanwhile, city staffers stuffed mailboxes and front gates with 1.3 million pamphlets in English and Spanish urging citizens to visit the PlaNYC website and submit their ideas on sustainability initiatives.

The most ambitious goal was to slash New York City's greenhouse gas emissions to 30 percent below their 2005 levels by the year 2030. City government would aim to cut its own emissions 30 percent below 2006 levels by 2017. A first-ever inventory of the city's emissions revealed that almost 75 percent of carbon dioxide came from heating, cooling, powering and lighting buildings. The other 25 percent came from transportation.

The remaining goals aimed to overhaul the city's transit system, bridges, water mains, power plants and building codes, and to do so in a way that protected water, air, land and other critical natural resources.

"Only five years ago, looking 25 years into the future might have seemed unimaginable," Bloomberg said in his speech, recalling the World Trade Center attacks. But now, with the city growing again, New Yorkers "have the freedom to take on the obstacles looming in the city's future, and to begin clearing them away before they become rooted in place."

Bloomberg pointed to the rise of unpredictable weather patterns and longer, hotter summers. "It's called global warming, but the impact can be local… To reduce the threat of dangerous storms, it's also essential that we do our part to dramatically cut greenhouse gases."

Some environmentalists criticized PlaNYC for not focusing more on climate change. Of the 10 goals, only one dealt directly with global warming: the promise to cut the city's emissions by 30 percent.

They also criticized it for not paying more attention to adaptation— the specific actions needed to protect residents and critical infrastructure from the impacts of climate change. The Village Voice newspaper pointed out the only speaker that day to raise adaptation as a concern was Cynthia Rosenzweig, the climate consultant from NASA.

If Aggarwala and the sustainability team thought the stretch of work from September to December 2006 was intense, the first four months of 2007 came as a harsh surprise.

Now that the sustainability office had laid out its goals, it had to figure out not just the types of projects the city could implement, but which city agencies would carry them out, where the funding would come from, and whether city or state legislation was needed to move forward.

The sustainability team had come up with 127 projects that would be divvied up among 10 chapters in the PlaNYC report, each reflecting one of the city's 10 sustainability goals.

As the plan took shape, the team began looping in Bloomberg at more regular and formal meetings.

Much of the talk centered on congestion pricing, which hadn't yet been discussed publicly. Doctoroff and Aggarwala pushed hard for the policy, which would charge drivers a fee to leave or enter Manhattan's business district during rush hour. But the mayor was still undecided. He was skeptical that such a policy could work or was needed in New York.

The question of money came up at almost every meeting. The city would need to commit about $1.6 billion to execute the plan over 10 years. At the end of the day, was the mayor going to say yes to it all?

The pace was frantic. People were exhausted and cranky. Some spent nights in their offices. At times they felt they'd never get all the work done.

Angela Pinsky, Doctoroff's deputy chief of staff who wrote three of the chapters, described a typical week during that period: "I'd wake up at 6 o'clock in the morning, go to work at 7 a.m., work until 11 p.m., go to my friend's house, drink a glass of wine, cry, and then go home and fall asleep, and then start again."

Still, like the others, she kept going. She said PlaNYC was the most meaningful project she had ever worked on.

Aggarwala described a similarly helter-skelter lifestyle. The refrigerator in his Hell's Kitchen apartment stood empty for nearly a year. He often skipped lunch, and his dinners tended to arrive in pizza boxes or paper cartons. He rarely saw his girlfriend, a resident in internal medicine at St. Vincent's Hospital Manhattan.

One afternoon at City Hall, Ariella Maron, who wrote five of the chapters, couldn't hide her weariness from Doctoroff.

"Dan comes over to me. He looks at me—my face is bloated, my shirt's wrinkled, I think my buttons were mismatched. And he sent me home. Here is one of the hardest-working men, who is known for driving staff really hard. This guy, who demands that everybody give their all, actually sent me home," she recalled, laughing.

Between January and March 2007, team members hosted 11 town hall-style meetings and gave 50 presentations to advocacy groups, community leaders and public officials. They sifted through more than 3,000 emailed suggestions from the public. "We saw where some of the concerns and fights were going to be, and there were a handful of things that we did differently as result," Aggarwala said.

It became clear, for example, that people thought the "green roofs" initiative, which would have covered rooftops with plants to absorb storm water and lower temperatures, was too expensive. So the team chose a cheaper alternative and urged New Yorkers to coat their roofs with heat-reflecting white or silver paint, which could lower household energy bills by as much as 25 percent. The city addressed the storm water problem by scaling up an existing program that turned concrete street islands into plant-filled patches that capture rain before it floods the sewers.

One of the most popular proposals was an initiative to plant one million trees throughout the city by 2030. The goal of Million Trees NYC was to improve air quality, provide cooling shade and beautify the urban landscape. But like every plan that changed the status quo in New York, there were complaints. People griped that trees provided unsavory pit stops for dogs and that tree roots could crack sidewalks.

To pay for the $400 million initiative, the city partnered with the New York Restoration Project, a nonprofit founded by entertainer Bette Midler that revitalizes neglected parks and open spaces.

That spring, Doctoroff, Aggarwala and a consultant from McKinsey briefed the mayor on the 127 initiatives in three separate hour-long sessions in the Bullpen.

"These were reasonably high-pressure, because this was the culmination of more than a year's worth of work. The mayor knew that," Aggarwala said. "The mayor asked questions and was engaged."

After the briefings, Bloomberg and Doctoroff often discusse(___ plan in private.

One of the biggest sticking points was congestion pricing. The mayor was still undecided.

Under the sustainability team's proposal, passenger cars entering or leaving some of Manhattan's most congested areas would pay $8 between the hours of 6 a.m. and 6 p.m. on weekdays. Commercial truck drivers would pay $21. Emergency vehicles, taxicabs and cars with handicapped license plates wouldn't pay anything.

According to the models the team had built, congestion pricing would reduce rush hour traffic by 6.3 percent and increase driving speeds by 7.2 percent. It also would bring in $420 million a year to improve and expand mass transit systems.

Some of the mayor's staff didn't think it was smart to take on such a contentious proposal. New York City needed the state legislature's permission to institute and collect the traffic fee. Getting that notoriously dysfunctional body to sign off on congestion pricing would be difficult. Drivers who commuted from outside the city wouldn't be pleased to pay, and state politicians wouldn't want to alienate those constituents.

To win that legislative fight, the mayor would not only have to be on board—he'd have to throw his political weight behind the plan. If it failed, his political reputation would be damaged and other important PlaNYC initiatives might be overshadowed or tainted.

"I think we were very honest about the risks of it getting done and what would happen at the state legislature," Doctoroff said of the conversations he and the team had with Bloomberg.

The mayor asked Doctoroff if it might be wise to shrink the size of the congestion pricing zone. The team mulled the idea, but stayed with the original proposal.

In the end, the mayor was swayed by the data. Bloomberg not only signed on, but also became one of the plan's biggest champions.

The Bloomberg administration chose a highly symbolic day to present PlaNYC to the public: Earth Day, April 22, 2007.

To meet the deadline, the team operated under the principle that "the perfect is the enemy of the good," Angela Pinsky said. "At some point you have to say, all we know that we can accomplish right now is that we can get someone who's smart and who can think about this problem and empower them."

That's how the team approached the chapter of the report they had recently decided to devote to climate change.

It didn't include building specific projects to help New York adapt to rising sea levels or the increasing frequency of especially severe storms. Instead, it offered three broad proposals.

The first goal was to create an intergovernmental task force to study potential climate impacts on critical infrastructure. The Department of Environmental Protection had already begun an adaptation study of the drinking water and sewage systems. Now subway tunnels, power plants, garbage terminals and other vital systems would get a look, too.

The second proposed developing individual adaptation strategies for the communities most vulnerable to coastal storms and sea level rise.

The third proposed a citywide assessment of the risks, costs and potential solutions for adapting to climate change. The city wanted floodplain maps to be updated regularly and building codes amended to account for increased flooding, higher winds and heat waves.

As the plan took shape, team members saw that they had created the beginning of a climate change strategy for America's biggest and most complex city. Climate change—like sustainability—was central to the agenda, not simply one of the 10 components, they realized.

"Virtually all of the 127 initiatives had some impact on [greenhouse gas] emissions," Aggarwala said. "You could read PlaNYC as a climate emissions plan, or you could read it as a broader sustainability or quality of life plan. I remember telling Dan [Doctoroff] it was like a telescope. We could look at it either way, and the best part was that we didn't have to choose between them."

With the Earth Day deadline fast approaching, crunch time set in. One day Maron took a cab home at 6:30 a.m. and showed up back at the office a few hours later, carrying a large iced coffee spiked with two shots of espresso.

Marc Ricks, who had helped hire Aggarwala and was now in charge assembling the final document, invited one representative from each city agency to come in and review their chapters before they went to print. He told them, "'Make all your changes in pencil. You don't get a pen. Only I have a pen,'" Pinsky said. "At some point you just have to shut it down."

A week before the launch, Aggarwala's team briefed the Sustainability Advisory Board on the plan's final details. In the seven months since its creation, the board had kept mum to the public on almost everything. Reporters' interviews with city officials and the board had "produced only vague whispers of what's coming, as if the city's next two-and-a-half decades are before a sequestered grand jury," the Village Voice said.

The board's silence had prevented a media frenzy over the plan's most controversial element, congestion pricing. The New York press had speculated for months over whether Bloomberg would or wouldn't go the way of London, with little indication as to which way he'd swing.

At a four-hour embargoed media briefing the day before the launch, Aggarwala finally answered the big question.

"It felt a bit like what it must feel like to come out of the closet on that Saturday, when, in front of the press, I could say, 'Tomorrow, Mayor Bloomberg is going to propose congestion pricing,'" he recalled.

The next day Bloomberg took the stage at the American Museum of Natural History in Manhattan. More than 700 guests crammed into rows of folding chairs arranged beneath the 21,000-pound model of a blue whale suspended from the ceiling. A massive video screen projected the mayor's image as he described the plan to create the world's "first environmentally sustainable 21st-century city" over the next quarter century.

Gov. Schwarzenegger offered his support in a taped video endorsement. With PlaNYC, "New York leaps to the forefront of cities dedicated to attacking climate change and protecting our environment," he said from the screen.

In another video, British Prime Minister Tony Blair called PlaNYC "a great act of leadership."

As Bloomberg rolled out the goals and initiatives, he reminded the crowd that the city's long-term population growth would "pose challenges that—if left unmet—could be paralyzing: Infrastructure, stretched beyond its limits. Parks, bursting at their seams. Streets, choked with traffic. Trains, packed beyond capacity. Dirtier air, more polluted water."

He added climate change to the daunting list. "As a coastal city, we're on the leading edge of one of the most dramatic effects of global warming: rising sea levels and intensifying storms. The science is there. It's time to stop debating it and to start dealing with it."

No city or country can solve global warming on its own, he said, but New Yorkers had a responsibility "to do our part and to show others it can be done in ways that will strengthen the economy's long-term health."

Finally, Bloomberg addressed what he called the "elephant in the room," congestion pricing.

"I understand the hesitation about charging a fee. I was a skeptic myself. But I looked at the facts, and that's what I'm asking New Yorkers to do."

Doctoroff, Aggarwala and the PlaNYC team watched from the front rows as the mayor laid out the vision they'd worked so hard to create. Pinsky peered at the faces around her—urban and regional planners, environmental activists, policy wonks, nonprofit leaders.

"This was a lot of stuff that they live to get governments to change. And it was hand-delivered to them," she remembered. "We were all crying."

The PlaNYC team knew the glow would be short lived. The opposition to congestion pricing would be especially fierce.

But for one day, at least, they and the mayor could celebrate.

Back at City Hall that night, the staff ordered take-out from the Kitchenette diner and waited for the press calls to start arriving. Then they headed home to sleep for the first full night in what seemed like years.

The next day, it was back to work for round two—the implementation of the plan.

"At what must have been 8:15 the next morning, I'm on my way to work, I get out of the subway, and there's an email from Dan (Doctoroff)," Aggarwala remembered. "It said, 'Congratulations. Now that you've had time to rest, how are you going to get this all done?'"

4

PREPARE FOR A FIGHT

In the months after PlaNYC's launch, the public and the media focused almost exclusively on congestion pricing, just as the Bloomberg administration had expected.

Much of the reaction was positive. The New York Daily News called congestion pricing the "wave of the future." The New York Times said it was "long overdue." "Yes! Yes! Yes! It's about time," a reader commented on a Times blog post.

But the negative voices were loud, too. Queens Chamber of Commerce president Raymond Irrera called it "a regressive tax that harms and could conceivably break the backs of small businesses and middle class residents that need to travel into Manhattan to conduct business." A Quinnipiac University poll showed that most New Yorkers opposed congestion pricing, even though 90 percent agreed traffic was a problem. Proponents cited their own poll that found New Yorkers favored congestion pricing when they were told of its benefits.

What mattered to the mayor's office wasn't the buzz, but the state legislature's reaction to the plan. They needed the legislature's blessing, and they needed it before June 21, 2007, when the lawmakers would recess for summer.

If New York didn't adopt congestion pricing that summer, it would lose out on as much as $500 million in grants from the U.S. Department of Transportation to help implement the plan. The mayor's office also wanted the program up and running as fast as possible, so it would be harder for the next mayor to shut it down.

The PlaNYC team began drafting a congestion-pricing bill to send to the legislature.

The mayor's lobbying team—led by Deputy Mayor Kevin Sheekey, Bloomberg's top political strategist—began meeting behind the scenes with policymakers from the city's five boroughs to explain the plan and its potential impact on traffic flows and air quality.

The mayor lobbied hard for it.

"The time for denial is over, the time for action is now. We are going to need Albany's help. I am going to campaign there. I would ask all of you to do the same thing," he told the Regional Plan Association, an independent urban research and advocacy organization.

A new study by a business group showed that traffic jams cost the metropolitan region $13 billion every year in lost business revenue, increased operating costs, decreased worker productivity and wasted fuel. If action wasn't taken, Bloomberg warned, commuters could some-day spend half of their working day stuck in cars during rush hour.

The Regional Plan Association and dozens of other civic, environmental, labor and real estate groups rallied behind the initiative. The Environmental Defense Fund and the Partnership for New York City produced a 30-second television ad supporting congestion pricing. They hired powerhouse lobbyist Patricia Lynch to push it in Albany.

Lynch was a former top aide to Assembly Speaker Sheldon "Shelly" Silver, the most powerful Democrat in the state legislature. He represented much of lower Manhattan, an area that would be heavily affected by congestion pricing. Two years earlier Silver had refused to back Bloomberg's plan to build a stadium to support New York's Olympic bid. But Silver hadn't taken a position on congestion pricing. Neither had Gov. Eliot Spitzer or state Senate Majority Leader Joe Bruno, whose support was also essential.

Bloomberg took his helicopter to Albany to meet legislators. The negotiations went well, but as evening loomed, the mayor's work wasn't finished. Bloomberg had to get back to New York, so he left Sheekey, his right-hand man, to continue the talks.

"So I get a hotel room at about 9 o'clock," Sheekey recalled. "I go to Target, I buy some new underwear, some socks, a dress shirt. And I get enough for just one day, because I was like, 'I'm going to go home tomorrow.'"

The negotiations dragged on for three nights, and Sheekey made more late-night shopping trips. "That's about as depressing as you can get," Sheekey said. "Buying underwear at Target in Albany at 9 o'clock at night."

Back in the city, Bloomberg showed off PlaNYC to the C40 Cities Climate Leadership Group, a global network of big-city mayors. His message resonated with the theme of the event: that cities—not federal governments or international councils—could lead the global fight against climate change. That was especially true in the United States, Bloomberg believed, given that Congress was unlikely to embrace any serious climate legislation.

A week later, the mayor appeared on NBC's "Today" show to plug another controversial initiative: a plan to convert the city's 13,000 yellow cabs to hybrids, which guzzle less gas than conventional cars.

"There's an awful lot of taxicabs on the streets of New York City obviously, so it makes a real big difference," he said. "These cars just sit there in traffic sometimes, belching fumes." He pointed to a yellow Ford Escape hybrid parked behind him. "This does a lot less. It's a lot better for all of us."

The hybrid taxi plan needed the approval of the city's Taxi and Limousine Commission, and opposition was sure to be fierce and unrelenting.

New York's powerful corporate taxi fleet owners, who have been called a "cabbie cartel," complained that hybrids had lower safety ratings than the trusty Crown Victoria sedans most drivers used. They also argued that the expense of buying and maintaining a hybrid would cut into drivers' take-home pay.

The Bloomberg administration had lined up some key endorsements, including Gov. Spitzer, City Council Speaker Christine Quinn and the New York Times editorial board. "We had every newspaper, every good government group, every environmental group, the public polls—everybody was in favor of it," the mayor recalled.

But "everybody" didn't necessarily include the state legislature.

Bloomberg took his helicopter to Albany again to try to broker a deal with Spitzer and Bruno, the Senate majority leader. The mayor sketched it out "on cocktail napkins left over from a take-in lunch of burgers and popcorn in Bruno's offices," according to Joyce Purnick, author of "Mike Bloomberg: Money, Power, Politics."

On June 21, the legislature adjourned without voting on congestion pricing. On July 16, however, it was introduced in a special session of the state Senate.

A grim-faced mayor sat with state senators in Albany in tense backroom meetings that ran late into the evening.

Democrats complained Bloomberg had failed to answer their basic questions about congestion pricing. The mayor was furious.

"Anybody that says we didn't have enough time to look at this is ridiculous," he shot back later on an Albany radio program.

"His posture was not ingratiating," state Sen. Kevin Parker, a Brooklyn Democrat, told the New York Times. "He says he doesn't know politics, and he certainly bore that out by the way he behaved."

Angry Senate Democrats voted as a bloc to defeat the measure. But Shelly Silver and some Assembly Democrats came up with a compromise that bought Bloomberg more time. The legislature agreed to create a commission to consider policies, including congestion pricing, to reduce New York City traffic. The legislature could then act on the commission's findings in the 2008 session.

The federal government cooperated, too, giving New York until the following spring to get the grant money. Proponents sighed with relief. "This is a tremendous breakthrough in the struggle to achieve a more efficient, mobile city," said Kathy Wylde, president of the Partnership for New York City, a business group and major backer of congestion pricing.

The PlaNYC team tried not to let the battle over congestion overshadow the rest of its agenda.

"We knew we had to keep the momentum going right away…and so we made an announcement, like, every week," said Ariella Maron, who was now deputy director of the Office of Long-Term Planning and Sustainability.

By July, nearly 70 schoolyards had been turned into green spaces, and a 13-agency task force had begun analyzing ways to manage the storm water runoff that routinely clogged the city's sewage system.

Bloomberg launched the Mayor's Carbon Challenge, which encouraged the private sector and institutions to voluntarily reduce their greenhouse gas emissions to 30 percent below 2006 levels by 2017—the target already set for city-owned buildings.

Two initiatives to curb carbon emissions from buildings—by far New York's biggest source of greenhouse gases—took effect. Biofuels would replace some of the heating oil in city-owned buildings, and new construction codes required all new buildings to have energy-efficient heating systems, light-colored roofs and other green features.

Outside the city, the mayor continued speaking about the need for climate action.

In a speech before the U.S. Conference of Mayors he pushed for a national carbon tax, which was gaining support among some environmentalists, business groups and former Vice President Al Gore.

"We have to stop ignoring the laws of economics. As long as greenhouse gas pollution is free, it will be abundant. If we want to reduce it, there has to be a cost for producing it," he said. "This is America! We can't be afraid to lead, to innovate, to experiment. Cities aren't afraid."

The speech drew special attention because Bloomberg had recently left the Republican Party and registered as an independent, a move many saw as a first step toward a 2008 presidential bid. His aides considered the speech one of the most significant policy addresses of his second term.

"The mayor likes big challenges," said Marcia Bystryn of the New York League of Conservation Voters. "Just by virtue of his personality, he likes to be in the lead. He likes the big idea."

That month, Bloomberg traveled to Bali, Indonesia to speak at the annual United Nations climate change conference. He used his speech to rail against the paralysis on climate action in Washington, D.C. He argued that city governments should have a seat at the climate-negotiating table, just like national and UN delegates at the conference.

"What I'm here to do is say cities are part of this, and New York City is doing its bit," he told CBS News.

Back home, things were looking up for the taxi initiative and congestion pricing.

The Taxi and Limousine Commission unanimously approved regulations that would effectively require more hybrid cars. And the state commission that was examining New York's traffic problem came up with a plan that was strikingly similar to the mayor's congestion-pricing proposal.

A Metropolitan Transportation Authority report said congestion pricing would contribute $4.5 billion to the MTA's capital spending plan for 2008 to 2013.

The legislature had until April 7, 2008 to decide whether to approve the plan. If it didn't, the city would lose its federal grant.

The deadline hung over the mayor's office like a dark cloud.

Bloomberg persuaded the City Council to adopt congestion pricing as a "home rule message"—a formal request by city politicians asking the state legislature to pass the plan.

But whether the message would resound in Albany was unclear.

Gov. Spitzer, who had backed congestion pricing in 2007, had resigned amid revelations that he was involved with prostitutes. Bloomberg immediately began lobbying Spitzer's successor, Lt. Gov. David Paterson, and within a week he had won Paterson's endorsement.

Bloomberg characterized opposition to his plan as stupid, sick and insane, according to the New York Times.

As the mayor rounded up supporters, one key politician still eluded him: Assembly Speaker "Shelly" Silver, whose decision would sway other Democrats on congestion pricing.

With the April 7 deadline just days away, the bill was introduced in the Senate, but not in the Assembly.

On the 7th, Silver emerged from a meeting to announce that the mayor's congestion-pricing bill "will not be on the floor of the Assembly." The bill didn't have anything close to a majority among Assembly Democrats, so why bother?

Bloomberg was outraged.

"It takes a special type of cowardice for elected officials to refuse to stand up and vote their conscience on an issue that has been debated ... for more than a year," he said in a statement that day. "Every New Yorker has a right to know if the person they send to Albany was for or against better transit and cleaner air. People know where I stood, and where members of the City Council stood. They deserved at least that from Albany."

Headlines on April 8 read like an obituary: dead, defeated, killed. The mayor's critics gloated at the dent to Bloomberg's political prestige. Many people assumed the much-lauded PlaNYC initiative was dead, too.

That morning, Bloomberg flew to Washington D.C. to give the keynote speech at Newsweek magazine's Global Environmental Leadership Conference. Sustainability chief Rit Aggarwala, who was on the plane with him, said there was no looking back for Bloomberg, no second guessing the wisdom of trying to get congestion pricing passed, no blame for the staff who had urged the mayor to risk the fight. "It's just not a Bloomberg thing to do that," Aggarwala said.

Instead, the focus was on the future. "We couldn't allow this defeat to stop us," Aggarwala said. "It was not at all easy to shrug off, but the importance of everything else meant it had to be."

5

ACCEPT IT, MOVE ON

In his speech in Washington, D.C. on April 8, 2008, Bloomberg didn't hide his bitterness over his loss in Albany. Legislators "didn't even have the courage to vote on it—they just killed it in a back room. That's not leadership," he said.

Congestion pricing was important, he added, "but let me make something crystal clear this morning. The other 126 initiatives are important, too, many of which … require no approval by any other level or branch of government."

The mayor's sustainability team moved a little more slowly over the next couple months, exhausted and drained by the loss of one of their most ambitious projects. They had launched many smaller initiatives during the congestion-pricing fight. Now, with just 18 months remaining in Bloomberg's second term, they had to rally again and get more initiatives into place to preserve their environmental agenda under future mayors.

In the Bullpen, digital countdown clocks bore the message "Make Every Day Count" and flashed red numbers reminding them of their deadline.

In May the City Council made the Office of Long-Term Planning and Sustainability a permanent fixture in the New York City bureaucracy. It also mandated that PlaNYC be updated every four years and codified the city's greenhouse gas reduction targets and water quality initiatives.

That summer, the city assembled a Green Codes Task Force, a group of 200 experts in design and construction who pored over 4,000 pages of building codes to find ways to make it easier to build green in the city. The mayor had already added sustainability measures to the codes. Now they were taking a deeper dive.

In September, the PlaNYC team took one of its most important and innovative steps: It formed the New York City Panel on Climate Change, an independent organization modeled after the Nobel Prize-winning Intergovernmental Panel on Climate Change. New York would be the first major city to produce its own climate projections—data that would inform policymakers about how climate change could impact the city's 520 miles of coastline.

At the same time, Bloomberg launched another group, the Climate Change Adaptation Task Force. It asked leaders from 40 city, state and federal agencies and private companies to figure out how to protect New York's critical infrastructure from the effects of climate change.

Not all of the sustainability office's plans were falling into place.

New rules to convert the city's taxi fleet to hybrids, for instance, hit a major roadblock. A taxi industry group filed a lawsuit in federal court to block the plan, which delayed the rules from taking effect on October 1 as scheduled.

The PlaNYC agenda, now one year in, was also the subject of scrutiny.

Some complained of what they saw as a gaping hole in the mayor's agenda: social equity issues in low-income neighborhoods. PlaNYC included plans for 165,000 affordable housing units, but a well-rounded growth agenda should go further, they argued. It should also improve access to quality education and health care and address homelessness and unemployment. "If sustainability is not just and inclusive, is it sustainable?" asked Tom Angotti, a professor of planning at Hunter College.

Environmentalists argued that Bloomberg wasn't moving quickly enough to revitalize the waterfront, improve regional parks and redevelop abandoned industrial sites. "Much still needs to be done," said the New York League of Conservation Voters.

For most New Yorkers, however, PlaNYC and the city's sustainability push was the last thing on their minds. They weren't thinking about going green, they were thinking about whether they'd soon be out of a job because of the growing financial troubles on Wall Street.

In March 2008, JPMorgan Chase acquired Bear Stearns for a fraction of what the global investment bank was once worth. Housing prices throughout the nation were sliding fast, with millions of homeowners defaulting on their mortgages. Wall Street firms watched the value of subprime mortgage securities—now deemed "toxic" assets—plummet.

Nowhere was this frenzied period of financial chaos more acutely visible than on Wall Street, the storied maze of cobblestone streets where Bloomberg made a name for himself in the 1970s as a bond trader.

On September 15, the financial services firm Lehman Brothers filed for bankruptcy, the largest filing of its kind in U.S. history. Overnight, 26,000 employees—many of them based in New York—were out of work, and millions of investors lost all or most of their money. Freshly unemployed bankers could be seen trudging aimlessly through the streets of Manhattan clutching cardboard boxes filled with the contents of their desks.

That same day, Merrill Lynch agreed to sell itself to Bank of America to stave off deepening financial troubles. On September 16, the federal government took over troubled insurance giant AIG with a $68 billion bailout. Banks stopped lending. Municipal governments, pensioners and families nationwide saw their assets shrink. Layoffs and penny pinching became the new normal as companies, governments and families struggled to meet their budgets.

With projected tax revenue plummeting, the Bloomberg administration faced a massive budget shortfall instead of the balanced budget it had enjoyed only a year earlier.

Instead of being crushed by the financial cataclysm, Bloomberg was invigorated as a politician. He had already put to rest rumors of a presidential run, and now he argued that as a former Wall Street trader and a self-made billionaire, he had the business acumen needed to lead New York City out of the crisis. On October 2 he announced he would run for a third term as mayor.

His announcement set off a raucous, citywide debate.

In the 1990s, New Yorkers had voted twice to limit mayors to two terms. Plenty of people and local politicians thought it should stay that way.

After heated arguments, however, the city council voted 29 to 22 to allow Bloomberg to seek re-election.

Bloomberg began shelling out millions of dollars of his own money to bankroll his campaign. His pledge to "steer the national conversation" about climate change was temporarily put on hold.

Carl Pope, executive director of the Sierra Club, had hoped to persuade the mayor to endorse his organization's new climate action campaign. But Bloomberg's people told him, "'No, no, no, we need to focus right now on the city," recalled Pope. "They didn't want him to make any new major commitments of his time outside of New York City."

As the re-election campaign began, the city's economic reality had flipped 180 degrees. The budget deficit reached $4 billion in 2009.

Of the PlaNYC initiatives, the high-cost transportation projects suffered most. The state-run Metropolitan Transportation Authority was facing a $1.2 billion budget deficit and didn't have the billions it had expected to collect from congestion-pricing fees. Environmental groups criticized the mayor for relying too heavily on that non-existent revenue to fund mass transit improvements.

A bus program that featured pre-boarding payment systems and bus-only lanes was delayed, along with construction on the seemingly eternally postponed new Second Avenue subway line in eastern Manhattan. Projects to more easily connect New Yorkers to regional transit networks also stalled.

The program to turn barren schoolyards into inviting playgrounds slashed its target of 290 plots by 12 percent. The plan to develop more "greenstreets"—the addition of small, rain-catching green spaces on streets and sidewalks—was cut in half. The timeline to build the afford-able housing units was pushed back a year.

But many of the plan's initiatives moved ahead, including one of PlaNYC's hallmark goals: to slash city government's greenhouse gas emissions 30 percent by 2017. Ariella Maron was plucked from the city's sustainability office to lead the plan from the Department of Citywide Administrative Services.

The Million Trees NYC campaign, which had already reached a third of its goal, continued.

Rit Aggarwala, who was still head of the sustainability office, credited Bloomberg for not scaling back more during this difficult period.

"I think you saw in a lot of other places that the green stuff was an option. It was a veneer. Therefore, when push came to shove, you put it aside," he said. "But the mayor knew how important this was" to the city's long-term economic development.

Bloomberg had another reason to push ahead on sustainability: the first report from New York's climate change panel was in and the results were unnerving.

By 2050, New York's average temperatures would likely rise 3 to 5 degrees Fahrenheit. Sea levels could rise by one foot, the panel warned. As a result of global warming, coastal flooding would be more frequent and severe. In the event of a hurricane, low-lying communities would be inundated with water much more easily than just a few decades ago.

The climate projections "put numbers to what we already know—climate change is real and could have serious consequences for New York if we don't take action," Bloomberg said when he announced the report.

Under this scenario, more than 100 types of infrastructure were at risk. Longer summers and more frequent heat waves would strain the electrical grid as New Yorkers cranked up the air conditioning. Higher average sea levels could increase erosion of beaches and salt marshes and speed the spread of pollution from industrial waste sites.

"Planning for climate change today is less expensive than rebuilding an entire network after a catastrophe," the mayor said. "We cannot wait until after our infrastructure has been compromised to begin to plan for the effects of climate change now."

Bloomberg also pressed ahead with what he hoped would become one of PlaNYC's crowning achievements: the Greener, Greater Buildings Plan.

The goal was to boost energy efficiency and conservation in New York's 26,000 or so largest buildings—nearly half the total square footage of all the buildings in the city. Many other U.S. cities required new buildings to be energy efficient, but New York would apparently be the first to impose stringent standards on existing properties.

The buildings plan wasn't nearly as controversial or politically galvanizing as congestion pricing. But it riled up the city's powerful real estate community, which said it was in the throes of the "most challenging economic climate in two decades."

The plan would create four laws. Building owners would have to meet strict energy efficiency standards for new construction and renovations and replace existing lighting systems with energy-efficient models. They also would have to track and report energy consumption for each building so the figures could be compared to similar buildings. Finally, they would be required to conduct energy audits every 10 years to identify energy-guzzling appliances or equipment and leaky doorways and windows. They'd then have to fix the inefficiencies if the improvements could pay for themselves in energy savings in seven years.

Relations between the building industry and the Bloomberg administration grew tense. Commercial property owners and housing cooperative "co-op" boards in particular said they couldn't afford to comply with such onerous rules at that time. Passing such laws in the midst of a credit crunch would be kicking a struggling industry while it was already down, they argued.

"The real estate industry was on its back, the construction guys were out of work. Nobody could get a loan. On its face, it was kind of improbable," said Aggarwala, who helped develop the plan from the sustainability office. "If you go read the headlines of what was going on [at that time], I mean, we were scared—everybody was scared."

Bloomberg believed the plan would not only reduce greenhouse gas emissions, but would also help get the city's economy get back on its feet. The building upgrades would stimulate private investment and create jobs, he said. Once the modifications were done, property owners would save a projected $750 million per year in energy costs.

An "extensive environmental agenda … is not bad for the economy. Being pro-environment and an activist in the environmental cause is good for the economy," the mayor has said.

Aggarwala met in March 2009 with Bloomberg and Robert Lieber, the deputy mayor for economic development. Lieber had recently received a letter from the Real Estate Board of New York expressing concerns about the plan. Given the pushback, he and Aggarwala wanted to make sure the mayor was still comfortable with moving forward on the proposals.

"The question was, 'Are we going to do this?'" recalled Aggarwala.

For half an hour the three men and a half-dozen other city officials sat at a round table in "the Cow," the second-floor room in City Hall whose formal name is "Committee of the Whole." Aggarwala walked the mayor through a PowerPoint presentation that gave an economic analysis for each of the four requirements.

Bloomberg made the point that getting a loan or paying for upgrades might be difficult now, but the economy would eventually recover. A short-term problem shouldn't determine the entire outcome of a long-term policy, he reasoned.

When the presentation was over, Bloomberg said, "Okay," Aggarwala remembered.

For a moment, Aggarwala and Lieber just looked at each other.

"'So we're going to do it?'" Lieber asked the mayor again.

"Yeah," the mayor said.

"All of it?" Lieber asked.

"Yeah!" the mayor said again, as if restating the obvious. Then he walked back to his desk in the Bullpen.

"We got the green light, and then we went and we did it," Aggarwala said.

On April 22—Earth Day, 2009—Bloomberg formally proposed the four green buildings laws.

The building industry challenged the initiative, as expected. Most of their objections centered on the fourth proposal—the one that required energy audits and related upgrades. Building owners feared they wouldn't have the upfront capital to pay for big fixes, even if savings were likely in the long run.

Throughout the summer and fall, the mayor's office, city council leaders and the building sector worked to hammer out a compromise. Finally they came up with a solution. Instead of doing expensive retrofits, building owners could meet about two dozen other, less cumbersome requirements, like sealing leaky windows and wrapping hot water pipes with insulating blankets. The Real Estate Board of New York was game.

"I think we got what was possible, and then some," said City Councilman James Gennaro, who participated in the negotiations.

As negotiations for the green buildings laws wore on, so did Bloomberg's election bid. The mayor hired a roster of political whizzes, spearheaded by his trusted adviser Kevin Sheekey, to handle the campaign, while he tried to stay out of the daily back-and-forth.

In September Bloomberg launched NYC Cool Roofs, which urged building owners to paint their rooftops with a reflective coating. The goal was to reduce energy consumption and air-conditioning expenses, thereby slashing greenhouse gas emissions.

"It's such a simple concept. Anyone who has ever gotten dressed in the summer knows it—light-colored surfaces absorb less heat than dark surfaces do," the mayor said at a splashy press event atop the YMCA building in Long Island City, a developing waterfront neighborhood in Queens.

New construction codes already required most new buildings to have reflective rooftops. Now existing buildings were being targeted, too, through a voluntary program.

To get property owners on board, the city mobilized a corps of volunteers. Bloomberg and former Vice President Al Gore were photographed on the YMCA's rooftop, roller brushes in hand. Gore drew laughs when he accidentally rolled his paint-drenched brush over the shoe of a Queens assemblywoman.

"The press had a field day" over the Cool Roofs project, Bloomberg later recalled. "They made fun of Al, they made fun of me. They made fun of the concept of painting your roof white."

Bloomberg didn't mind the jokes. People liked the initiative, he said, because they saw they could benefit from participating. "They're the ones saving money."

By October 2009, environmentalists were praising Bloomberg's long-term vision and his use of the bully pulpit to make sustainability part of the public discourse. Bloomberg was a "rock star mayor" for putting his sustainability plan "in the DNA of government," said one London-based climate advocate.

Community groups were less enchanted, according to the New York Times. A Harlem-based environmental justice group complained that smaller buildings were still allowed to burn the dirtier heating oils that spewed asthma-causing soot into the air. Others complained that the city's use of artificial turf—not grass—in new sports fields built under PlaNYC contradicted the mayor's call for more green spaces.

Bloomberg, as it turned out, would have four more years to hash out these issues.

On November 3, he was narrowly elected to a third term, making him only the fourth mayor in New York history to serve three consecutive four-year terms. He spent a record $102 million of his personal fortune on the campaign, about $175 per vote.

Ariella Maron recalled the moment when the digital countdown clocks in her office near City Hall dialed back another four years. "You know, I used to love the countdown clocks ... then I really started to hate the clocks," she remembered, laughing. "Because your mind is preparing for a sprint, and all of a sudden you realize, 'Oh, this is a marathon.'"

Maron, who was then 33, said she and some other women on the staff had been waiting until Bloomberg left office to start having children. "You're too busy to have a family," she explained. "Then it's like, 'Wait a second—four years?' The biological clock is ticking!'"

With a third term in the bank, Bloomberg again focused on the global climate stage. The U.S. House of Representatives had passed a sweeping cap-and-trade bill, but its prospects for surviving in the Senate were dim. The mayor's conviction deepened that real action on climate change would come from cities—not state or federal governments or international organizations.

Bloomberg also believed that progress would be faster if climate change measures were presented as public health initiatives.

Using cleaner heating fuels reduced asthma rates as well as carbon emissions. Improving water networks provided cleaner drinking water while also making cities more resilient during storms. Initiatives that benefit people today are more likely to succeed than something like cap-and-trade, whose full effects won't be realized for generations, he believed.

"You, me, our children are breathing this air. You, me and our children are fighting the effects of congestion," the mayor has said. "I've always thought that if we focus on the short-term, rather than the long-term effects on the planet, you will get to the same place, but you'll get to it without an awful lot of the naysayers, and you'll get there without an awful lot of the delays that people put in."

Bloomberg took that message to the 2009 United Nations climate change conference in Copenhagen, Denmark. New York's sustainability plan was featured in an interactive exhibition called "Future City." The mayor spoke at a reception for 100 mayors from around the globe.

"We were there, to some extent, to proselytize around what we were doing [with PlaNYC]," recalled Sheekey, who accompanied the mayor on the trip, along with Rit Aggarwala.

But as the focus in Copenhagen turned to the international climate talks, which had been going on for years without reaching a binding agreement, the mayor grew impatient. World leaders shuffled around in an endless cycle of meetings, none of which seemed to be bearing fruit. Three days into the two-week conference, Sheekey said Bloomberg told his team, "'You know what? I think we're done … let's get back to the airport. We're going to go home now.'"

"And we went home, because we realized there was nothing else to do," Sheekey said.

6

DIG IN

The idea for what would become one of PlaNYC's most visually dramatic initiatives was brewing in New York while Bloomberg was still at the Copenhagen climate summit.

On a gray, chilly day in late 2009, Andy Darrell, New York regional director for the Environmental Defense Fund, was studying the sweep of glassy skyscrapers and boxy beige buildings from the window of his seventeenth-floor office in central Manhattan. Thick plumes of black smoke coiled up from the tops of the buildings, as they often did. But this day, for some reason, Darrell and one of his colleagues took notice and asked, *What is that gross stuff?*

The "gross stuff" turned out to be emissions from high-sulfur Number 6 and Number 4 heating oil blends.

The two oils were being burned in about 10,000 city and privately owned buildings, including the office tower on Park Avenue South where Darrell worked. Although these buildings represented just 1 percent of the city's building stock, they produced more soot than all the city's cars and trucks combined. Soot is a major public health hazard, because it easily enters the lungs and bloodstream, causing childhood asthma, heart attacks and premature death.

Darrell's epiphany led the Environmental Defense Fund to produce a report calling for a citywide phase-out of Number 6 and Number 4 oil. Darrell is on the PlaNYC Sustainability Advisory Board, so he raised the issue at the group's meetings. The city health department was also concerned—it had just released a study linking the two heating oil blends to severe air pollution. The seeds of what would become the NYC Clean Heat program had been planted.

The start of Bloomberg's third term in 2010 saw a sweep of changes in the administration. Rit Aggarwala, the first director of the Office of Long-Term Planning and Sustainability, moved to California so his wife could finish her medical training at Stanford University. Aggarwala was replaced by David Bragdon, who had overseen environmental programs as president of the Oregon Metro Council.

Bloomberg, meanwhile, was taking on new leadership roles in his push for action on climate change. The U.S. Senate had pulled the plug on a sweeping cap-and-trade bill, and conservative Republicans were downplaying the scientific evidence of climate change. With the prospect of passing meaningful legislation dimmer than ever, he was sure that progress would come outside of Washington.

"We have to do something about it now," Bloomberg said at an energy conference. "Sitting around and arguing about what it's going to be like 50 years from now is not the kind of way I want to spend my time."

By this time, Bloomberg had incorporated sustainability and climate initiatives into his private company, Bloomberg LP. The financial data giant was greening its buildings worldwide. It had also begun measuring the environmental impact of the businesses tracked in its data system, information that would be valuable to socially responsible investors.

Internationally, Bloomberg zeroed in on the C40, the international consortium of big cities whose members were taking action to reduce greenhouse gas emissions. But the C40 was struggling to secure a steady financing stream and a professional staff. The Clinton Foundation's climate initiative was providing help, but only for specific projects.

The mayor wanted to head the organization. He made an argument similar to the one he had used in his last mayoral campaign—that his data-driven approach to planning could make the C40 a more effective policy tool.

The C40 steering committee elected Bloomberg as chairman in September.

Bloomberg said his election reflected the impact PlaNYC was having on other cities. "I think it says a lot about the kind of changes we've been able to affect here," he said at a news conference.

But the New York Times pointed out that Bloomberg had recently pledged to give the C40 nearly $20 million of his foundation money over three years. Bloomberg "essentially muscled aside the Clinton staff members working on the projects," the Times said. It quoted a Clinton advisor who said, "What are we going to do, fight him? They have the money; the golden rule applies"—as in, he who has the gold, rules.

Bloomberg ignored the squabble. Instead, he pulled out his check-book again and pledged $50 million to the Sierra Club. The money would be used to jumpstart the Sierra Club's Beyond Coal campaign, which aimed to shutter one-third of America's 500 coal-fired power plants and replace them with natural gas and renewable energy.

Like the Sierra Club and some green groups at the time, Bloomberg saw natural gas as a "bridge fuel" that could replace coal until enough renewable energy was available. Natural gas produces about half as much carbon dioxide as coal when combusted.

But many other environmental groups opposed the expansion of gas drilling, because it has been linked to water and air contamination. Many worried that the gas boom would ultimately do more harm than good for the climate.

Bloomberg's critics complained he was hypocritical. The mayor wanted natural gas for New York City, but only if it polluted someone else's groundwater, they claimed, since Bloomberg strongly opposed gas drilling in the city's upstate watershed.

The mayor shrugged off the detractors. He believed his gift would help save more lives than any other policy he has backed, aside from his 2003 ban on indoor smoking. By dramatically slashing greenhouse gas emissions from coal, "you are really impacting the world—not just New York City and America."

"These things have to be looked at in the context of, 'What are the alternatives?'" he has said. "We're not going back into the caves without electricity and cooking our meals over a few logs. We are going to use energy. And the bottom line is that wind and solar are great, but they just do not have the potential at the moment to become the main source of energy in our country. And so we've got to make a decision here."

Bloomberg's $50 million pledge to the Sierra Club came with a caveat: The group first had to rigorously analyze its anti-coal campaign strategy. His foundation offered technical support. "I'd never seen anything like this in the nonprofit world at all," said Carl Pope, the Sierra Club's chairman.

The mayor brought a similar degree of rigor to his new post with the C40. One of his first acts was to commission a detailed survey of the C40's effectiveness. It revealed a host of weaknesses—including lack of financing, skilled staff and global collaborations—and sparked talks of combining the C40 with the Clinton Foundation's climate initiative. The groups merged in 2011.

The C40's nearly 60 member cities have since adopted initiatives that will allow them to reduce their combined carbon dioxide emissions by 240 million tons per year by 2020—about 35 times the amount of annual U.S. emissions.

Cities had to do much more than simply curb their emissions, Bloomberg believed. They also had to focus on protecting themselves from the impacts of climate change.

The need for a more resilient New York City came squarely into focus in August 2011, when Hurricane Irene swirled its way up the East Coast.

The weather forecast was so ominous that Gov. Andrew Cuomo and the Metropolitan Transportation Authority shut down the city's subway system for the first time in history. Bloomberg issued an unprecedented mandatory evacuation order for some 370,000 residents in low-lying areas.

The mayor had learned the hard way what happens if you underestimate a storm.

Eight months earlier, the sixth largest snowstorm in New York's history had buried the city in four-foot drifts at Christmas. Public transit ground to a halt and snowplows couldn't get through the clogged streets. While the city struggled, Bloomberg was reportedly at his mansion in Bermuda. He didn't reappear in public in New York until a day later.

Now, with Hurricane Irene approaching, Bloomberg "wanted to go from bozo of the blizzard to hero of the hurricane," Doug Muzzio, a political science professor in Manhattan, told the New York Daily News.

Instead, Hurricane Irene made Bloomberg the butt of a new round of jokes. It brought heavy rains and caused power failures and flooding, but not the widespread devastation officials had feared.

Although most New Yorkers applauded Bloomberg's better-safe-than-sorry precautions, people whose homes had been looted or vandalized during their evacuation were angry. The Daily News teased Bloomberg for his "sky-is-falling act."

Other extreme weather events hit the city that year, each one triggering new speculation about climate change. January 2011 was the snowiest January on record. July and early August saw 16 blistering days of 90-degree-plus heat. August was New York's rainiest month ever.

"Over the past year, New Yorkers have had a taste of what climate change may mean for our city," Bloomberg said in a speech at Climate Week NYC. "Perhaps such extreme weather events are merely coincidental. Or perhaps they're warnings of what the future holds—unless we act now. With the stakes as high as they are, just doing nothing is no option."

Although Hurricane Irene had largely spared New York City, it exposed the city's vulnerabilities and offered a glimpse of what could have been. It didn't look good.

The city's Economic Development Corporation, or EDC, revamped its emergency response plans for the 20 million square feet of city-owned properties it manages, including piers, parking garages, rail yards and food distribution centers. "We, like a lot of New Yorkers, went through a dress rehearsal with Irene," said EDC president Seth Pinsky.

New York was now more than four years into its PlaNYC agenda. The plan had been updated the previous spring to include a chapter on solid waste and recycling. PlaNYC now had 132 initiatives to roll out, up from 127.

The city was showing signs of a dramatic physical transformation.

About three-fourths of flat rooftops were coated with heat-reflecting paint to lower air-conditioning bills and curb carbon emissions. That, plus other measures, had reduced greenhouse gas emissions 13 percent.

More than 6,000 garbage trucks, police cars and other city-owned vehicles had been swapped for hybrid or natural gas vehicles. Close to half of the yellow taxi fleet was also hybrid—up from just 3 percent in 2007—even though the U.S. Supreme Court had struck down the city's plan to require all the 13,000 cabs to be hybrids. Opponents had successfully argued that the taxi rule was a de facto regulation of emissions standards, a power only the federal government holds.

The five boroughs were greener and leafier thanks to the Million Trees NYC program.

"If you go around the streets of New York, you can see it. You can feel it," said Kevin Sheekey, who had left the mayor's office to head government relations and communications at Bloomberg L.P.

Less obvious were the beginnings of the city's $1.5 billion Green Infrastructure Plan to improve water quality by keeping storm water out of sewage systems and waterways. The green plan would cost less than traditional "gray" infrastructure projects, said Cas Holloway, the environmental commissioner who spearheaded the plan.

Porous sidewalks replaced solid concrete slabs. Rooftops were fitted with rainwater collection barrels and grassy gardens. Tree pits and parking lots were reconfigured to serve as natural storm sewers.

The industrial waterfront was also being transformed into public spaces and parks built to withstand sea-level rise and coastal storms.

Brooklyn Bridge Park, once a cluster of piers covered with warehouses and semi-trucks, was now a stretch of grassy lawns, athletic fields and gardens. More than a dozen wetlands in the Bronx, Staten Island and Queens were being restored so they could once again act as natural buffers against storm surges and floodwaters.

Along Broadway, the once-controversial pedestrian plazas were filled with people who could relax and enjoy the city in a completely new way.

Shopping was up. Vehicle exhaust fumes and neighborhood air pollution were down. San Francisco, Washington, D.C., Boston, Philadelphia and Chicago were building similar plazas.

"You're starting to see people use the city a little differently," Janette Sadik-Khan, the city's transportation commissioner, has said. "I think it's been really profound in terms of how we get around the city."

Part of the difference was the hundreds of miles of new bicycle lanes being built through PlaNYC to make it safer for people to take to two wheels. Sadik-Khan helped create a bike share program, paid for by the financial firm Citigroup and dubbed Citi Bike, which would soon fill Manhattan and Brooklyn streets with 6,000 cerulean blue cruisers.

People loved—or hated—the bike lanes and bike sharing with equal fervor. Early critics said the program amounted to a massive advertisement-on-wheels for the banking industry, which they blamed for the recession. But Bloomberg refused to be swayed. Citigroup was footing most of the bill, and the plan fit well with PlaNYC's goal of reducing air pollution from cars.

In 2012, another initiative was struggling to get off the ground—the NYC Clean Heat campaign, the project inspired in part by the thick, black smoke outside Andy Darrell's office at the Environmental Defense Fund.

The city had ordered buildings that burned Number 6 and Number 4 heating oil blends to switch to cleaner fuels by 2030. The rules covered the smaller buildings that environmental justice groups had complained were excluded from earlier initiatives.

But many building owners and developers said they couldn't afford to make the switch. Changing heating fuels required expensive new equipment and, in some cases, the installation of new natural gas pipelines.

To get the program moving, city officials worked with the Environmental Defense Fund and other groups to compile the addresses of each of the roughly 10,000 buildings that burned the dirtier heating oil. Then they worked with the buildings' owners to find ways to meet the rules.

The solution that emerged was a public-private partnership to help finance the upgrades. In June private banks pledged to lend building owners $90 million to convert to cleaner fuels. The city pledged an additional $23 million for mixed-income residential buildings and to cover some of the banks' losses from missed loan payments. Natural gas utilities promised to upgrade some of their infrastructure and to offer incentives that would make it easier for buildings to comply with the rules.

The collaboration reminded Darrell of the early days of the PlaNYC Sustainability Advisory Board, when disparate groups sat down together to hash out solutions to difficult problems. He said Bloomberg's personal involvement in the Clean Heat initiative helped pull it together.

"When the mayor says, 'No, we're going to have one more meeting on this,' people show up at that one more meeting. What are you going to do, say no to the mayor?" Darrell said. "And then you go, and you realize maybe there is something we can work on. And the table will continue on its own a little bit."

In October, David Bragdon, the sustainability office director, left to head a wetlands revitalization project in Queens. Bloomberg appointed Sergej Mahnovski, the city's director of energy policy, to take over PlaNYC.

Mahnovski's transition wouldn't be smooth. A hurricane was forming in the Caribbean. His new desk would temporarily be at the city's emergency management headquarters in Brooklyn.

7

FIND LESSONS IN THE STORM

O n October 11, 2012 a single wave of low pressure off the west coast of Africa traveled across the Atlantic Ocean, forming a system of clouds, wind and rain. As the storm hit the Caribbean, it gathered size and strength from the area's warm waters.

On October 24, the storm developed an eye—officially making it a hurricane. The World Meteorological Organization named it Sandy. After slamming into Jamaica, Cuba and the Bahamas, Hurricane Sandy turned northeast, running parallel to the eastern shoreline of the United States.

Scientists were conflicted about what would happen to Sandy as it moved north. European weather models showed it running straight toward New York and New Jersey. The U.S. National Weather Service projected it would move out to sea.

On the second floor of City Hall, Bloomberg met daily with his senior staff and city commissioners to discuss what to do. Representatives of the National Weather Service, the Metropolitan Transportation Authority and the state Department of Health were also in the room. For more than a decade, scientists had warned that New York was extremely vulnerable to a severe climate change-fueled storm. Bloomberg and his staff had taken note, but so far they'd focused primarily on lowering greenhouse gas emissions to fight global warming. They were just beginning to focus on adaptation—physically protecting the five boroughs from climate-related disasters.

If the European models were correct, the city would be hit, and hit hard. People in low-lying areas would have to be evacuated.

If the Weather Service was right, however, the storm would probably miss New York, and thousands of people would be needlessly forced from their homes, as they'd been a year earlier for Hurricane Irene.

As Sandy rotated up the coast, it collided with a low-pressure system that energized it and pushed it toward New York. The collision also changed the structure of the storm, transforming it from a hurricane into an extratropical cyclone. It measured more than 1,000 miles in diameter, making it the largest cyclone in recorded history at that time. Instead of Hurricane Sandy it was now Superstorm Sandy.

The urgency of the City Hall meetings increased. What had been hypothetical questions a few days earlier were looking more and more like realities. How long would it take to evacuate people from low-lying areas? When should they shut down the transit system? Should hospitals in vulnerable locations be closed?

On Friday, October 26, Bloomberg held his first news conference about the storm, urging New Yorkers to monitor the forecasts and "prepare themselves by stocking up on basic supplies." He moved his staff, including the Office of Long-Term Planning and Sustainability, from City Hall to the Office of Emergency Management headquarters in Brooklyn. It had been built after the 9/11 attacks destroyed the previous command center near the World Trade Center and was equipped with the latest technology, including back-up generators and direct feeds to TV news channels.

By Sunday morning, all the storm models agreed that Sandy was headed straight for the tri-state area. The mayor, flanked by City Council Speaker Christine Quinn, Police Commissioner Raymond Kelly, and other key members of his administration, issued mandatory evacuations for low-lying areas.

Because the storm was going to arrive at high tide, Coney Island, the Rockaways, lower Manhattan, and parts of Brooklyn and the Bronx could be hit with "a surge from six to 11 feet," Bloomberg said. "This is a serious and dangerous storm ... We'll certainly get through this, but we'd like to get through this with nobody getting hurt, and that's a lot more important than property damage."

If New York was going to flood, one of the first places the water would go was the city's vast network of subway tunnels that crisscross the five boroughs and run under the major rivers—crippling the primary mode of transportation for more than eight million people. In 2011, Columbia University geophysicist Klaus Jacob, who was also a member of the city's scientific climate change panel, had published a report detailing the damage infrastructure would suffer from a major storm. It included maps showing exactly where the water would go and how quickly it would get there.

Using the report as their guide, transit employees rushed into the vulnerable tunnels and removed costly, sensitive electronics that would be destroyed if submerged in salt water. They moved subway cars and buses to higher ground.

Jacob, meanwhile, was busy preparing his own home for the coming deluge. He and his wife had bought the house in Piermont, N.Y., 12 miles north of the city, knowing it was susceptible to climate-related flooding. They had raised the foundation, but local zoning laws allowed them to lift it only 6 inches above the 100-year flood zone—not nearly enough, Jacob knew, to protect it from a storm as big as Sandy.

Jacob asked members of the Piermont Rowing Club, where his wife had been a member, to help him lift the stove and dishwasher onto the kitchen counters and carry rugs and furniture to the second floor. Then he led the rowers from house to house, helping his neighbors do the same.

Back in the city, most waterfront residents were heeding Bloomberg's call to evacuate. But many stayed, hoping Sandy would spend her fury elsewhere. On Sunday and Monday, as the forecasts became more alarming, some of the stay-behinds tried to flee. But the roads leading away from the ocean were already clogged with traffic or partly submerged from Sandy's early storm surge.

Across the city, grocery and corner store shelves lay bare. Families filled bathtubs with water and placed flashlights by their beds. Bloomberg cancelled school. Businesses shut their doors. The MTA halted subway and bus service. New York, the city that never sleeps, fell eerily quiet as it waited for the storm to arrive.

At 7:30 p.m. on Monday, Superstorm Sandy made landfall in Brigantine, N.J., 120 miles south of New York City. Eighty mile-per-hour winds hurled boats onto front lawns, crumpled beachside buildings and flooded the streets with three feet of water.

Over the next few hours Sandy coiled up the coast and into New York City. People watched from their windows as their streets and neighborhoods crumbled and flooded. Trees collapsed into buildings and onto cars. Inundated with salt water, a transformer erupted into a ball of sparks and left a large swath of lower Manhattan dark. A construction crane atop one of the city's tallest skyscrapers dangled dangerously above West 57th Street. Water poured down stairs and into subway tunnels, smashing metal gates as it rushed in.

Thousands of low-income residents were stuck in public housing built in low-lying areas. The backup power supply at NYU Langone Medical Center in Manhattan failed, forcing doctors to deliver babies by iPhone flashlights. Hundreds of patients had to be evacuated in the middle of the storm.

Charlene Davis, who is partly paralyzed and uses a wheelchair, watched Sandy roll in from her living room window in the Brooklyn neighborhood of Coney Island, just a few blocks south of the Atlantic Ocean. Water from a nearby inlet crept up the front lawn, engulfing waist-high shrubs. Her teenage son and daughter threw their weight against the front door, trying to keep it from gushing inside. But the force of the water pushed an air conditioner through the back window of the townhouse.

The children carried their mother upstairs. The family rode out the remainder of Sandy in a second-floor bedroom that they lighted with scented candles. Downstairs, Davis' wheelchair floated in five feet of water, along with her hospital-style bed, television, pots and pans.

As the water infiltrated electrical systems, it sparked fires across the city. In Breezy Point, a small community at the tip of the Rockaway peninsula, 130 houses burned to the ground. A smaller fire in the Belle Harbor section destroyed about a dozen houses.

The storm surge pushed north up the Hudson River Valley, flooding Piermont and other waterfront towns. While Klaus Jacob and his wife slept, the first floor of their home filled with two feet of water.

Not until the wind and rain moved north on Tuesday morning, and New Yorkers emerged from their homes, did Sandy's true toll become apparent. Thousands of buildings sat submerged in water, sand, and toxic muck dredged up from the New York Harbor seafloor. Millions of people were without power, heat or running water. Bloomberg's city, which was just beginning to emerge from the recession, was facing billions of dollars in damage.

Bloomberg and his staff had spent almost six years immersed in data showing that such a storm was possible, but the extent of the damage still shocked them.

"It was a wake-up call for just how vulnerable we are," Bloomberg said.

8

SEIZE EVERY OPPORTUNITY

As New Yorkers dug out from Sandy, environmentalists and pro-climate action politicians outside the city seized on the tragedy as a cautionary tale of what Americans could face if carbon emissions continued unchecked. Forty-four New Yorkers died and thousands of homes had been destroyed. The city suffered nearly $20 billion in economic and physical damage.

"If there was ever a wake up call, this is it," Bill McKibben, an environmental writer-turned-activist, told the daily newscast Democracy Now.

"Climate change is no longer some far off issue," Rep. Ed Markey (D-MA) wrote in the Huffington Post. "It is at our doorstep ... We can't wait for the next disaster to take action to cut the pollution that is changing our weather for the worse. We need to act now, before more lives are lost, and more livelihoods are ruined."

Scientists are usually reluctant to attribute specific weather events to global warming, but most agreed that the strength, size and destructive force of Superstorm Sandy were likely fueled by above-average ocean temperatures caused by rising greenhouse gases. Some hypothesized that Sandy had turned toward New York and New Jersey, instead of curving out to sea, because record-low sea ice in the Arctic was altering the movement of the atmosphere.

o pointed out that sea level is seven inches higher than
ago, making it easier for Sandy's storm surge to breach
and flood communities.

Until Sandy arrived, the issue of climate change had largely been absent from the 2012 presidential election. For the first time since 1988 it hadn't been mentioned in any of the presidential debates. But now, with the election just a few days away, global warming was at the fore-front of voters' minds.

President Obama was a well-known proponent of climate action, although environmentalists were frustrated that he hadn't accomplished more in his first term. The Republican candidate, Mitt Romney, had helped launch the nation's first cap-and-trade program when he was governor of Massachusetts, but he had since reversed his view that U.S. carbon-cutting policies could help slow global warming.

For Bloomberg, there was a sense of "I told you so," said Kevin Sheekey, the mayor's former political strategist. "Everyone sort of woke up with Sandy and said well, yeah, this can really impact us. Mike Bloomberg had been talking about that since 2007."

On November 1, Bloomberg unexpectedly endorsed Obama.

"The devastation that Hurricane Sandy brought to New York City and much of the Northeast—in lost lives, lost homes and lost business—brought the stakes of next Tuesday's presidential election into sharp relief," he wrote in an editorial published in the opinion section of Bloomberg News. "[Climate change] is too important. We need determined leader-ship at the national level to move the nation and the world forward."

That same day, the mayor's weekly news magazine, Bloomberg Businessweek, hit stands with the headline "IT'S GLOBAL WARMING, STUPID" splashed across the cover in bold, black letters. Below was a photograph of a flooded and darkened lower Manhattan.

Josh Tyrangiel, the magazine's editor, tweeted, "Our cover story this week may generate controversy, but only among the stupid."

As power and services were slowly restored, New Yorkers, too, began reflecting on the storm's connection to climate change. A poll by Siena College found that nearly 70 percent of city residents believed the super-storm was linked to global warming.

"Sandy was in some ways a wake-up call on these issues, an unfortunate one," said Andy Darrell of the Environmental Defense Fund. "It brought home to people the very basic feeling that energy, water, climate change, all of these things matter in a very visceral, very real way to the city—not just to the city as a future city in 50 years, but right now. Getting it right now is important."

As city workers and community organizations picked through the rubble, they found that small pockets of New York had managed to escape the worst of the storm—many of them the direct result of projects inspired by Bloomberg's sustainability push.

The 1.3-mile Brooklyn Bridge Park, one of PlaNYC's green space initiatives, had emerged intact. The park's rolling berms had helped keep the storm surge from entering nearby neighborhoods. When the water receded, the park's salt marsh plants and rugged outdoor furniture bolted in place looked much the same as they did before. Sandy was a test of the park's design goals—and it passed.

A $54 million project to restore and enhance wetlands across the city had produced benefits as well. Wetlands in Soundview Park in the Bronx and Freshkills Park in Staten Island helped hold back and absorb the floodwaters, allowing the communities behind them to stay relatively dry.

A privately designed residential development in the Rockaways also came through unscathed. When Arverne by the Sea was expanded in 2007, the developers included a strip of grass-covered dunes and plants to slow down and break up any incoming storm surge. They also elevated the buildings and installed hurricane-grade windows. The houses, which have steel frames and cement-composite shingles, sit above empty underground chambers designed to redirect storm surge.

Except for a few missing shingles, the latest section of the development was fine. Like the rest of the Rockaways, it lost power. But because its elevated electrical systems didn't flood, its power was restored days before other buildings in the neighborhood.

These success stories were small and few. Despite six years of sustainability initiatives, New York hadn't done much to physically protect the city from climate change-related threats.

Some people chastised the Bloomberg administration for focusing on reducing greenhouse gas emissions instead of building sea walls and levees. But the PlaNYC staff and volunteer experts were unapologetic. Adaptation work takes more time and money than mitigation, they said, and such large-scale, large-cost projects can be a difficult sell to the public.

"I was realistic enough not to have unrealistic expectations," said Klaus Jacob, the geophysicist who served on the city's climate panel and saw his own home flooded by Sandy. "Engineered measures such as sea walls, berms, levees, and raising of structures … take many years if not decades to finance and implement."

Sandy pushed that work to the top of the city's priorities list. Bloomberg and his top officials decided that New York needed a climate change-focused rebuilding plan, one that would not only help New York recover from the storm, but rebuild stronger and smarter so it would be better prepared for future climate threats.

"We knew that in order to even answer this question, we were going to have to figure out a way to dedicate resources to it, independent resources," recalled Cas Holloway, the city's deputy mayor for operations. "We wanted it to be a serious, well-resourced, but also expeditious effort. PlaNYC took 18 months. We didn't have that kind of time."

They already had a team of scientists ready to go in the form of the New York City Panel on Climate Change. They also had the infrastructure in place to develop a report, thanks to their work on PlaNYC.

What they didn't have was time. Bloomberg wanted the plan done by June so his administration could start implementing the proposed solutions before he left office.

In late November, Seth Pinsky, president of the city's Economic Development Corporation, was at home with his wife, Angela, and newborn son when he got a call from Robert Steel, deputy mayor for economic development, asking if he would lead what would become known as the Special Initiative on Rebuilding and Resiliency, or SIRR.

Pinsky's immediate reaction was to say no. His son was just two weeks old, and his EDC work kept him so busy that he was already concerned about not spending enough time with his family. He and his wife had both worked on PlaNYC and they remembered vividly the toll it had taken on their personal lives.

But as Pinsky thought about the job, he realized how important it was for the city. "What better way to honor the future of my son than to start thinking about the city I hope he grows up in and lives in the rest of his life?"

Marc Ricks, Dan Doctoroff's former chief of staff, was tapped as second in command.

Like Pinsky, Ricks had worked on PlaNYC and was hesitant to commit. He was working at Goldman Sachs as the vice president of infrastructure, and he was happy in his job. He called former Deputy Mayor Doctoroff, his mentor and friend, to ask his opinion. Doctoroff encouraged him to say yes. Ricks accepted the offer the next morning.

That afternoon, Ricks and Pinsky met with Bloomberg's speechwriter to craft how the mayor would announce SIRR the next day. They would keep up that frenetic pace for the next seven months.

Bloomberg announced the ambitious undertaking in a conference hall at the Marriott Downtown before hundreds of environmentalists, city officials, community leaders, businesspeople and members of the press. The hotel had flooded during the storm, and the mayor could see the waterline on the wall.

For 40 minutes, he talked about SIRR, which he said would build on his administration's previous work with PlaNYC. This initiative, however, was focused solely on preparing the city for climate change-related disasters. It would identify the city's vulnerabilities and find ways to fix them.

"The city that we know today exists, I think it's fair to say, only because the New Yorkers who came before us responded to tragedy and adversity with inspired vision and impressive resolve," he said. "Adapting to climate change is a citywide challenge, not just a coastal challenge. We have to reexamine all of our major infrastructure in light of Sandy—and how we can adapt and modernize it in order to protect it."

With 520 miles of waterfront to protect, SIRR would be a massive undertaking. Some of the projects they had in mind, like building protective sea walls and dune systems, would disrupt neighborhoods and in some case change the patterns of people's lives. And the price tag wouldn't be cheap.

Sandy, however, had been an incredible motivator. New Yorkers had lost their sense of security in the storm and were desperate to get it back. Their anxiety gave Bloomberg and his staff the leeway to push their climate agenda far beyond what they imagined possible, and far beyond what any other city in the world had done.

"Unfortunately it takes a Sandy-level event to prompt the institutional will to take big steps," Ricks said.

9

RACE TO THE FINISH

In a high-rise a few blocks from City Hall, about 30 people gathered on Jan. 2, 2013 to begin creating the plan that would help New Yorkers rebuild homes and businesses damaged by Superstorm Sandy and prepare the city for future climate-related disasters. Some of them knew each other. Others didn't. Each had been recruited because of his or her very specific skills in energy, policy, infrastructure, the economy or climate change.

Seth Pinsky and Marc Ricks, the project's leaders, had spent a month selecting the people they wanted and persuading them to say yes. Many had to quit or take leaves of absence from high-profile, high-paying private sector jobs.

"There is a real sense of civic pride among New Yorkers," Pinsky said. "People recognize that [Sandy] was an unprecedented event in the city's history and they really wanted to contribute to the recovery."

At that first meeting, Pinsky laid out the team's strategy. Bloomberg wanted the plan to focus not just on protecting New York from the next Sandy, but from any other climate change threats that lay ahead.

The project was framed around three questions: What happened during Sandy and why? What could happen in the future because of climate change? What, specifically, should be done to prepare for those possibilities?

"It was a very simple, but very powerful way of organizing our work and our thinking," Ricks said.

Ricks tried to prepare the team for the personal sacrifices they'd have to make to get the project done on time.

"I told people you get to have work and one other thing," he said. "I said for me, it would be work and my family. That I have two small kids. For you maybe it will be work and the gym. Or work and your friends. Or work and sleep. That is all you are going to have time for. And that proved to be true."

The countdown clocks prominently displayed in City Hall were constant reminders of how little time the group had. If they met their June deadline, Bloomberg could build momentum behind the report and start implementing some of its suggestions before he left office on December 31. If they didn't, the plan could easily be shelved by the next administration, possibly led by a mayor with less interest in climate change.

"We were very conscious that if we do not get this out ... then it is not going to be worth the paper it is printed on because the next team will just come in and say," never mind, said Cas Holloway, the deputy mayor for operations.

The team worked six to seven days a week from January to June. People canceled vacations, skipped family events, declined wedding invitations. They slogged through sicknesses and holiday weekends. Some weeks, workdays stretched to 15-plus hours.

Each team member was allowed one taxi ride a day, usually when working extremely late or extremely early. One employee's expense sheet was kicked back because he took two taxi rides in a single day. When asked to explain, he said he took a cab home at 4 a.m. and another back to work at 7a.m.

"It was an incredibly intense process," Ricks said. "Everybody made sacrifices. My three-year-old learned how to say things like, 'Daddy, I don't want you to go to work. It is Sunday. You don't work on Sunday.'"

More people were added to the team as the months passed. The SIRR staffers crisscrossed the five boroughs to meet with experts in insurance, utilities, hospital management, telecommunicatioɪ portation and other fields.

As the plan took shape, they held dozens of public forums in neighborhoods hit hardest by the storm—areas that would be most affected by the plan—to get residents' ideas and hear their concerns. At one meeting, people stressed the importance of hiring workers from the neighborhoods where sea walls or other major projects would be built. SIRR staffers took these suggestions back to their colleagues and reshaped the plan accordingly.

Meanwhile, Bloomberg created another volunteer group—the Building Resiliency Task Force—to produce a report that would be useful not just to New York, but also to cities around the globe. Led by the nonprofit Urban Green Council, 200 real estate experts, developers, attorneys and engineers came up with ideas to make new and old buildings more resilient in extreme weather events. The group swapped research and ideas with the SIRR team, sometimes even sharing staff.

The Sustainability Advisory Board, the group of disparate business, political and environmental interests that had been deeply involved in PlaNYC, was briefed twice by the SIRR team, and some members consulted on the project.

"The timeframe and urgency [of SIRR] … just didn't leave as much time for the level of formal consultation that was incorporated into PlaNYC," Ricks said. "We drew on a number of experts, but by and large it had to be of a more ad hoc nature."

One of Pinsky's first steps was to reconvene the city's climate panel, which was now an official part of the New York City government. To create an aggressive rebuilding and resiliency strategy, his team needed the latest scientific projections. The panel's last report had been published in 2010—and a lot had happened in three years.

The nearly two-dozen scientists gathered every Friday in a NASA conference room above Tom's Restaurant at West 112th Street and Broadway, the diner made famous by the Seinfeld comedy series. Those who couldn't attend in person called in to a speakerphone set up in the middle of the room.

"For the scientists, Hurricane Sandy didn't end," said Cynthia Rosenzweig, who co-led the panel. "From January until June it was basically 24/7. It was doing science in real time."

The panel set three research goals: How is New York City already being impacted by climate change? What will the next half century look like? How will New York City's 520 miles of coastline be affected?

Climate projections are usually done on regional scales, areas measuring hundreds of miles. But the SIRR team needed hyper-local information. Instead of how much the sea will rise along the entire East Coast, it needed to know how much it will rise in New York Harbor, or along the Rockaways.

To do this, the scientists made adjustments to the climate model used by the Intergovernmental Panel on Climate Change for its latest global warming assessment. By tweaking the model, they were able to develop projections for a 100-mile radius around New York City for the next 40-some years. They wanted to look further into the future, but just didn't have the time. They modeled two different emission scenarios: In one, global greenhouse gas concentrations stabilized after 2100 because world governments had substantially reduced their carbon emissions. In the other, emissions continued to rise, unchecked.

In either scenario, the future looked daunting.

By the 2020s New York City could be an estimated 3 degrees Fahrenheit warmer than it is today, the panel discovered. By mid-century, it could be 6.5 degrees Fahrenheit warmer. New Yorkers currently deal with an average 18 days a year where temperatures breach 90 degrees Fahrenheit. By 2050, that could jump to 57 days—nearly two full months.

Also by mid-century, nearly one-quarter of the city could be in a floodplain, with large, heavily populated swaths of Brooklyn, Queens and Staten Island prone to frequent widespread flooding. Intense hurricanes would hit the city more often, as would extreme winds and heavy rain events.

New York City has already experienced sea level rise nearly twice the global average since 1900, climbing 1.2 inches per decade. The situation appeared even bleaker as the scientists looked ahead. By the 2020s, New York Harbor would likely rise four to eight inches, or as much as 11 inches in the worst-case scenario. By the 2050s, sea level would rise 11 to 24 inches—or maybe as much as 31 inches.

This added ocean height would be disastrous for New York. If the sea rises higher, even a storm much smaller than Sandy could cause the same amount of damage.

The scientists' briefing sessions with the SIRR team turned into crash courses on climate science, modeling and interpreting projections.

To Bloomberg, science was the backbone not only of SIRR, but of all the environmental work his administration had done in the last six years.

"What we've tried to do with all of these things is have some real science, not just say something because you read it in the paper or it would be fashionable to say," he said in an interview. "I think—I hope—every single thing we've done can be justified based on real research and real numbers."

Bloomberg was involved in the resiliency strategy from start to finish. Pinsky and his staff constantly briefed the mayor on the initiatives they were proposing and how those initiatives might be funded. As the release date neared, the meetings became more frequent and lasted longer.

"The mayor is certainly like all people, and has evolved in his time in office," Pinsky said. "What I think is more striking is the consistency of his approach... He is not interested in getting into a discussion about whether climate change exists, but instead really focuses on what it means and what we need to do about it. He is willing to take on controversy if it's for the right policy reason, but he also expects that what is proposed is based on detailed and rigorous analysis. That was true during PlaNYC and that was true during this special initiative as well."

On June 11, 2013, seven and a half months after Superstorm Sandy slammed into New York, Bloomberg unveiled a 438-page, $19.5 billion plan to prepare the city for global warming—the fruit of all the work done by the SIRR team and the many people who helped in the effort. He spoke at a refurbished warehouse in the Brooklyn Navy Yard with the East River, the Williamsburg Bridge and the Manhattan skyline behind him. City staffers, scientists, community organizers and reporters packed the room.

Bloomberg looked at ease behind the microphone, a slight smile forming as he talked. With just six months left in office, the plan would be the finale to his climate change agenda.

"Six years ago, PlaNYC sounded the alarm about the dangers our city faces due to the effects of climate change today, including the worsening impacts of extreme weather," Bloomberg said. "Since then, we've done a lot to attack the causes of climate change and make our city less vulnerable to its possible effects … But Hurricane Sandy made it all too clear that no matter how far we've come, we still face real, immediate threats."

For the next 45 minutes, the mayor laid out the plan for a massive overhaul of New York City's transportation, energy, parks, building and insurance programs, as well as a sweeping coastal protection system. SIRR included 257 initiatives spread across the city's five boroughs.

The projects ranged from complex to easy. Some needed city, state or federal laws. Others, private-sector cooperation. Some required massive construction projects while others could be implemented quickly. Almost all of them needed funding.

Among the proposals was $1.2 billion in financial incentives for businesses and homeowners to stormproof their buildings by lifting them out of flood zones, moving electrical equipment to higher floors or using durable materials. One initiative called for the city to work with the Federal Emergency Management Agency to update flood insurance maps. Another called for more changes to zoning and construction codes, so new structures would be built with climate change in mind.

SIRR called for diversifying the city's energy supply and incorporating more renewables, so utility companies could restore power faster after a disaster. Public housing, much of which was flooded during Sandy, also should be modified to withstand future storms.

Some of the biggest and most expensive projects were part of the proposed coastal protection system. The 37 projects included constructing a system of levees and floodwalls along Staten Island's eastern shore, as well as building dunes and restoring wetlands throughout the five boroughs. Lower Manhattan would be protected with levees, deployable floodwalls and flood-tolerant landscaping.

SIRR also created recovery plans for the five neighborhoods hit hardest by Sandy: the Brooklyn-Queens waterfront, the eastern and southern shores of Staten Island, Southern Queens, Southern Brooklyn and Lower Manhattan. The plans laid out how Sandy had damaged each community and how climate change would affect that community in the future. Then it offered plans to prepare for those problems.

To pay for the $19.5 billion plan, the city had already secured nearly $15 billion in federal relief money and in city capital improvement funds. That left a $4.5 billion funding gap that it hoped to fill with federal, state or private grants.

Bloomberg also announced the creation of a new position: Director of Resiliency for the City of New York.

"We can't completely climate-proof our city," Bloomberg said. "That would be impossible. But we can make our city stronger and safer—and we can start today ... We've got a plan. We know what needs to happen. And we know it can't wait."

As Bloomberg pushed away from the podium, the audience stood and applauded.

Dozens of SIRR staffers and scientists joined the ovation, their exhaustion temporarily replaced by pride and satisfaction. They had produced one of the world's most aggressive and scientifically accurate climate resiliency plans—and they had done it in an extraordinarily short period of time.

They were also aware, however, of the tenuousness of their achievement. The plan would take decades to complete. The Bloomberg administration would have six months to start the work, but it would be up to the next mayor, or perhaps the next several mayors, to see it through.

10

FIGHT FOR THE FUTURE

Like anything new in New York, Bloomberg's post-Sandy rebuilding and climate resiliency plan has been both lavishly praised and sharply criticized.

The public generally likes SIRR. According to one poll, 74 percent of New Yorkers favor the plan, and 52 percent believe it will protect the city from future storms and flooding. Dozens of local green and community groups have also expressed their support.

The plan has been praised internationally as well. Political leaders and climate activists around the globe have commended Bloomberg for taking such a strong stance on climate change and for acting so quickly after Superstorm Sandy.

"I think it would be hard to be more comprehensive than New York," said Heather McGray, co-director of the vulnerability and adaptation initiative at the World Resources Institute. She said the plan is considered one of the most aggressive global warming strategies in the world.

Still, questions have been raised about SIRR's $19.5 billion price tag and about the feasibility of its most ambitious projects, particularly the coastal protection system. Others question whether it accurately portrays the risks climate change poses to America's biggest city.

Anthony Watts, a well-known climate skeptic and blogger, called the plan "Bloomberg's Climate Fantasy." The Heartland Institute, a libertarian think tank partly funded by billionaires David and Charles Koch, said SIRR is built on faulty science.

Some of the researchers who worked on SIRR think it doesn't go far enough. Because the report was done so quickly, the New York City Panel on Climate Change could only complete global warming projections to the mid-21st century. But that time frame is too short, many say, given that the projects built under the plan's recommendations will have to survive far longer than 40-some years.

"Look around," said geophysicist Klaus Jacob, a panel member. "New York City is filled with buildings and systems that were put in place 100-plus years ago. This means that whatever projects are being proposed will be around for a long time."

Scientists are especially concerned about Bloomberg's determination to continue developing New York's 520 miles of coastline, much of it wetlands filled in over the centuries to accommodate new neighborhoods. These areas, including Manhattan's heavily populated Lower East Side, were among the first to flood when Sandy hit.

Even with the complicated coastal protection system envisioned by SIRR, scientists say these low-lying areas could still flood if another Sandy-like storm hits New York. And as sea levels rise, even smaller storms could someday cause as much damage as Sandy did.

"At some point, I suspect we'll have to abandon at least some areas," said Philip Orton, a physical oceanographer at the Stevens Institute of Technology in Hoboken, N.J. who consulted on the panel's latest projections. "There'll be no other choice."

State and city officials appear split on what to do with the waterfront.

Gov. Andrew Cuomo created a $400 million land-buying program that pays clusters of homeowners in the most vulnerable areas the pre-Sandy values of their houses. The collections of homes will be torn down and the property left vacant to act as a natural buffer for future storms. Hundreds of homeowners on Staten Island have applied for the program, including nearly all of the Oakwood Beach community on the island's eastern shore.

Bloomberg, on the other hand, believes the waterfront shouldn't be abandoned. "It's one of our greatest assets," he said when he unveiled SIRR. "We must protect it, not retreat from it."

With that in mind, Bloomberg has proposed a different land-buying program that would pay homeowners the post-Sandy value of their houses. Unlike Cuomo's program, it would buy individual plots, not just clusters of properties. Instead of leaving the properties vacant, however, it would sell the land to developers or individuals who would assume all future risks.

Sandy victims themselves are divided over what to do about the waterfront areas.

Donna Crockett, a nurse and retired New York City police officer, wants to leave her home in Howard Beach, Queens, just blocks from Jamaica Bay, a major inlet of the Atlantic Ocean. During Superstorm Sandy her family fled to the roof to escape rising floodwaters. They'd like to take advantage of the buyout programs, but can't because they are reserved for higher-risk oceanfront neighborhoods. They've applied for rebuilding funds, but haven't yet received enough money to fully repair their house.

"If the city offered to buy my house, I would do it," Crockett said in August, when the air in her living room was still thick and damp from mold. "I used to love the ocean, but now I see the wickedness of it."

Scott and Stacey Nagel, who live about 10 miles from the Crocketts on the Rockaway Peninsula, say they will never abandon their neighborhood.

Sandy sent seven feet of water into their basement, destroying their college-age son's bedroom. The house sagged so much that they had to install scaffolding to keep it from collapsing. The couple has paid about $120,000 out of pocket to repair the house, but more is left to be done. Their insurance company is offering $90,000 at most.

The Nagels like to say that they, like many in the Rockaways, were born with sand between their toes. "We're not leaving," Scott Nagel said. "We just need to be better protected."

The question of what to do with the waterfront is one of the many climate issues New York City's next mayor, Bill de Blasio, will face when he moves into City Hall on January 1—if, that is, de Blasio decides to tackle climate change at all.

The mayor-elect has said he supports Bloomberg's environmental and climate change initiatives and has called SIRR a "bold blueprint" for protecting New York from global warming threats. But de Blasio has also tried hard to distance himself from Bloomberg. After 12 years in office, and several controversial decisions, including a highly criticized stop-and-frisk police policy, Bloomberg has developed a somewhat toxic reputation in New York. His work on climate change is barely recognized, even by the media that has been evaluating his tenure.

Some worry that de Blasio might decide to scrap PlaNYC and SIRR in favor of creating his own plan, even though scientists say such a delay would be dangerous and costly.

The Bloomberg administration has done what it can to require future mayors to deal with sustainability and global warming. The New York City Panel on Climate Change is, by law, an official part of the city administration and is legally required to update its global warming projections at least every three years. Another law requires the Mayor's Office of Long-Term Planning and Sustainability to continue working on climate change resiliency.

But whether these efforts will be enough to ensure the survival of the Bloomberg administration's work is unclear.

"We'll keep providing the science no matter what, but we have no control over whether the next administration will pay attention to the work," said Cynthia Rosenzweig, co-leader of the climate change panel. "It could very well fall on deaf ears."

The Bloomberg administration is still trying to implement as much of SIRR as possible before the de Blasio administration begins. Of the 59 initiatives they set out to finish by the end of 2013, they had completed, or nearly completed, three-fourths of them by November. The projects range from approving construction codes that force builders to develop with climate change in mind to dumping 1.2 million cubic yards of sand—enough to fill the Empire State Building—onto beaches destroyed by Sandy.

But none of SIRR's major initiatives, like sea walls, are underway. And the administration hasn't plugged the $4.5 billion funding gap.

"There's so much more to do," he said during his interview in September with InsideClimate News. "When you write the history, I'd like to think we play a decent part. I would hope that whoever comes after us does a lot more. I'm going to live here; my kids are going to live here. You would hope that's just the beginning, and that we've maybe provided the blueprints."

Bloomberg plans to continue his work on climate change after his term ends on December 31. He is going to stay involved with the C40 Cities Climate Leadership Group. He has also recently announced a project with billionaire-turned-climate activist Tom Steyer and former Treasury Secretary Henry Paulson to calculate how much money climate change will cost the United States in coming decades.

But these initiatives focus on climate change at the national or international level—not New York City where Bloomberg's name might do more harm than good.

Some of the people and organizations that worked with the mayor on sustainability and climate change initiatives are under no such constraints. For more than a year they've been meeting privately to make sure PlaNYC and SIRR live on.

"We want to find a way to take the things that are working and carry them forward, and then improve and fix the things that aren't working—or add to it things that haven't even been thought of yet," said Andy Darrell, who served on the PlaNYC advisory panel and is one of the coalition's organizers.

Their mission is two-fold. They want to keep City Hall connected to experts in climate change modeling, green buildings and energy infrastructure. And they want to make sure the diverse group of New Yorkers who helped shape PlaNYC stay seated at the same table.

"One of the most important things underlying all of PlaNYC was that table," Darrell said. The priority now is "keeping that table going and making sure that the chairs are representative of what New York City is."

But the issue remains whether New York, or any other city for that matter, can persist with such a costly and complex undertaking without a powerful, strong-willed leader guiding the show—a Michael Bloomberg, if you will.

"You gotta lead from the front," Bloomberg said in September, as the City Hall countdown clocks marked off his final days in his cubicle in the Bullpen. "Nobody is going to start it from the grassroots. The public's not going to say, 'Oh, I want to raise my house. I want to pay more taxes.' It's not going to happen. That's what an executive's job is … That's the way democracy really works."

ABOUT THE AUTHORS

Katherine Bagley reports for *InsideClimate News* on the intersection of environmental science, politics and policy, with an emphasis on climate change. Her work has appeared in Popular Science, Audubon and OnEarth, among others. She holds master's degrees in journalism and earth and environmental sciences from Columbia University.

Maria Gallucci is a journalist in New York City and a former clean economy reporter at *InsideClimate News*. She previously lived and worked in Mexico City and is a graduate of Ohio University's E.W. Scripps School of Journalism.

InsideClimate News is a Pulitzer Prize-winning, non-profit, non-partisan news organization that covers clean energy, carbon energy, nuclear energy and environmental science – plus the territory in between where law, policy and public opinion are shaped. Visit us at www.insideclimate-news.org and to make a fully tax-deductible donation, visit https://donatenow.networkforgood.org/1439575

An interactive version of this book, with photos, video, timelines and documents is available on our app, ICN Books.

Made in United States
North Haven, CT
03 June 2022

19737316R00049